A Young Person's Guide to Military Service

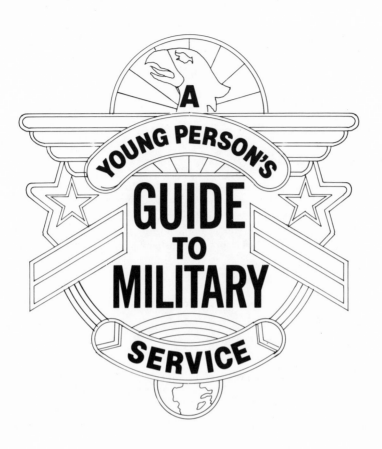

A YOUNG PERSON'S GUIDE TO MILITARY SERVICE

Jeff Bradley

Foreword by U.S. Sen. Paul E. Tsongas

THE HARVARD COMMON PRESS
Harvard and Boston, Massachusetts

The Harvard Common Press
535 Albany Street
Boston, Massachusetts 02118

Printed in the United States of America

Library of Congress Cataloging in Publication Data

BRADLEY, JEFF, 1952–
    A Young Person's Guide to Military Service
                        /2/83   H.S   8.95
    Includes index
    1. United States—Armed Forces—Vocational
guidance
I. Title.
UB323.B7   1983   355'.0023   82-23343
ISBN 0–916782–31–X
ISBN 0–916782–32–8 (pbk.)

Illustrations by Chris Van Dusen
Cover design by Peter Good

10   9   8   7   6   5   4   3   2   1

To Marta

Contents

Foreword

PEOPLE ARE DRAWN to the U.S. military for various reasons. Some are inspired by its great moments of heroism and glory, from Valley Forge to Iwo Jima. Some simply need a job; today the military maintains 2.1 million Americans in uniform, while another million are in the reserves or the National Guard. Whatever the reason, most every red-blooded American youth feels at least a twinge of interest, at one time or another, in joining the service. I was no exception.

In my second year of law school I began to wander into the library stacks to read about guerrilla fighting in Indochina during World War II. By the end of the year I had decided to leave law school and join the Special Forces as a medic. I would work in a village, I thought, helping to protect its inhabitants. The year was 1966, and the war in Vietnam was in full swing.

While still dreaming of valor in rice paddies, I had a chance meeting with Jack Vaughn, then the director of the Peace Corps, who tactfully let me know I was crazy. He caused me to reassess what I would find in the Army once I signed up. My military career ended before it began.

Because I had a pie-in-the-sky notion of what soldiering was all about, joining the Army would have been a mistake for me. I would have been a very disillusioned soldier. But many have found a home in the military; for some it is the break of a lifetime. The important task for all young persons thinking of enlisting is to soberly assess their expectations and the likelihood of fulfilling those expectations in the military.

There is much to assess. Since the advent of the all-volunteer force in 1973, the options have become more numerous—and more complex. Not only are there four branches of the military to choose from, each with pluses and minuses, there is a range of other choices to face: enlistment terms that vary from two to six years; training programs that offer pay, bonuses, and educational benefits; and overlapping concerns such as job assignment, military unit, and geographical placement.

Further complicating the young person's decision is the constantly changing character of the military itself. The army of Beetle Bailey and Sergeant Bilko is adapting to the high-technology weapons and the all-volunteer force. As the armed forces have changed to attract and retain the kind of specialized manpower they require, many old military stereotypes have become invalid. Junior enlisted personnel, for example, earn dramatically higher pay than they used to, are more apt to be married, and, if single, are more likely to live off base. The military is more than ever an institution in flux, especially for groups like women and blacks. What was true yesterday is not necessarily true today.

A book that debunks the myths and dissects the choices is of obvious value to anyone contemplating military service. Jeff Bradley's guide, with its clean writing style and consistently sensible advice, is bound to open eyes. And a wide-eyed look at the military is what prospective recruits need.

As readers of this book make their final choice, they ought to figure in the balance the value of national service for its own sake. The military offers tangible rewards such as job training, money toward college tuition, and so on. But military employment is unlike the usual kind—say, a job at an auto shop or the corner grocery. A stint in the military is service to a higher cause: the defense of our nation. The war in Vietnam hurt the image of military service as a patriotic endeavor, and to some extent a stigma persists. Many important consequences have followed the Vietnam debacle, but a lesser regard for national service ought not be one of them.

Though I have never served in the military, I spent two years as a Peace Corps volunteer in Ethiopia. It was the formative experience of my life. After twenty-one years in which my farthest trip had been to Annapolis, Maryland (where the Dartmouth swim team competed against the Navy), I found myself in an Ethiopian village seventy-five hundred miles and several cultural light years away from home. The challenge of cross-cultural sharing with the Ethiopians was formidable.

But working and living in Ethiopia brought me great satisfaction, much of which arose from the sense of being part of a worthy cause larger than myself. This, above all, is what voluntary national service can offer young people.

No one, however, ought to plunge into voluntary service of any kind without weighing the options carefully. This principle applies especially to military service, where a signature on a dotted line can mean an irreversible commitment for six years and the risk of combat.

SEN. PAUL E. TSONGAS

Preface

THERE IS A RENEWED INTEREST in military service in this country. Recruiters are having no trouble meeting their quotas, service academies are enjoying an upswing in applicants, and Reserve Officers' Training Corps is growing. All this seems to be happening for several reasons. For one thing, the young people who are entering the armed forces have few—if any—memories of the war in Vietnam. Economic conditions are playing a major role, too, leading some people to charge that an "economic draft" is in effect. Finally, each branch of the service is spending millions of dollars on sophisticated advertising campaigns that hold out the promise of jobs, education, and adventure.

Whatever the causes, as more and more young people look at the armed forces they find two general sources of information: the military itself and various antiwar groups, both of which take a relatively one-sided approach. According to recruiters, a tour in uniform can be the best thing that has ever happened to you. You can serve your country, make money, learn a trade, get an education, and do interesting things in exciting places. The antiwar groups claim you'll become a mindless cog in an imperialistic military machine, an object of abuse from your superiors, and a killer of innocent civilians.

A more realistic picture of life in uniform lies somewhere in between. Larry Anderson of the Harvard Common Press came up with the idea for this book, and it became my task to chart a path between the proponents and opponents of military service. I wrote neither to persuade people to join the armed forces nor to keep them out. The message of this volume can be expressed in one sentence: A six year commitment is a long time; make sure you know what you are getting into. I have tried to stress the advantages as well as the disadvantages, the attractive offers and the catches in each of them.

To accomplish this I talked to military personnel from Pentagon officers down to recruits fresh out of basic training. My sources ranged from a career Army officer who proudly stated that "the Vietnam experience was the most real thing in my life" to an attorney who got out of the Air Force as a conscientious objector. Between these extremes were veterans, childhood friends who are or were in the military, and other individuals in every branch of the service.

The factual information in this book comes from government documents and conversations with recruiting personnel in each branch. Because certain programs are constantly changing I have included only the ones that are likely to be in effect when this book is published.

I received enormous help from military officials as well as civilians. Some provided information, some patiently explained complex matters, and others checked over sections of the book for accuracy.

I am particularly grateful to the following: for the Army, Maj. Lars Hedstrom, Col. John Grant, Kirk Hazlett, Dennis

Cokenour, Lt. Col. William Knapp, Joan Orth, George Patzurakis, Capt. James Symmonds, Col. Gary L. Werner, Denis Keating, and Sgt. Lee Gates.

For the Navy, Capt. Jim Hitchborn, PO Ray Harris, Lt. Comdr. Kenneth Pease, CPO Dick Murray, Harold McClung, Lt. Comdr. Tim Wyld, Yeoman Luella Harvell, and Anna Urband.

In the Marines, Capt. Jim Hitchborn, Midshipman Third Class Stan Dietrich, Staff Sgt. Harry Boniface, Capt. Guy Durand, Lt. Col. W. S. DeForest.

For the Air Force, Charles Chandler, Will Ketterson, Ann Blanchard, Richard Howlands, Lt. Col. Marv Harris, Capt. James Jarell, Capt. Neal Bierbaum, Maj. Joe Purka, Lt. Col. Eric Solander, and Staff Sgt. Gail Lewis.

In the National Guard, Sgt. Major Ray Roy.

For the Coast Guard, MCPO Bob Bonnette, Lt. Comdr. Dan McKinley, Lt. Joseph Loadholt, Comdr. Thomas Watkins, Bob Scheina, Lt. JG Stephen Jackson, and Capt. R. T. Getman.

Bettie Sprigg of the Department of Defense helped a great deal, as did Rev. James Bank, Steve Olsen of the Boston Public Library, Cynthia Toomer of the Harvard Libraries, and Ed Santella, an attorney who specializes in military matters. Bob Abernathy also shared his experiences with me.

A word of sympathy must go to the students in my expository writing classes at Harvard University, who patiently sat through countless examples of how to write that centered on military and recruiting situations.

This book was written in about the same time it takes a person to go through Marine boot camp. Kathleen Cushman and Linda Ziedrich whipped this manuscript into shape as thoroughly as any drill instructors, and Richard Marius recruited me for the Harvard Common Press.

1. Thinking about the Military

FOR MOST YOUNG PEOPLE, life seems to be a bowl of choices. You are faced with decisions on what classes to take, what schools to attend, when and if to get married, and what sort of work to choose. Many of these decisions are interrelated, and none of them are easy.

If you ever listen to the radio, watch television, read magazines, or look at billboards, you find yourself hit with another set of choices: these involve military service. The Army, Navy, Air Force, Marine Corps, and Coast Guard are spending over $120 million per year to get you to think about joining up.

You see the ads everywhere. Some promise jobs, others stress dollars for education, and some push "the adventure of a lifetime." After a while it begins to sound like you can join up and become a fighter pilot, get paid to go to college, learn a trade that promises a lot of money, and have a wonderful time doing it all.

Often the ads focus on a particular problem of yours. If you have been looking at a college catalog and trying to figure out where you will get the money to pay for your schooling, your ears perk up when they talk about cash for education. If you're stuck in a low paying job and have no marketable trade, you listen when they talk about job skills. And if you're tired of home and sick of school and bored with your town, you dream of going to places like Europe, Hawaii, or the Far East.

You begin to think about getting into the military.

If you tell anyone what you're thinking about or ask them for advice, you'll probably get an earful. Whether they've been in uniform or not, almost everyone has an opinion about the armed forces. Many people think the military is somehow good for you. Others express shock that you want to have anything to do with the armed forces, a group they associate only with death and destruction. And your friends may laugh at the thought of you doing pushups while wearing a uniform and short hair.

They've all got something to say and a clear idea of what you should do with the next few years of your life. But it's *your* decision, and there are a lot of things to consider as you make it. Military service can be a very satisfying experience with some distinct benefits. Joining up can be the first step in solving some of the problems in your life. But it can also be an enormous source of frustration and unhappiness. Once you are in uniform the military has control over you—more control than you may have bargained for.

Weighing the Advantages and Disadvantages

Joining one of the armed forces may very well be a good way of straightening out your life. On a very basic level the military can remove some of the hassles of your day-to-day existence. When you join up they take you in and give you new clothes, a clean place to live, and plenty of food that you don't have to cook or pay for. If you get sick or need to see a dentist, it doesn't cost you anything. No one ever claims that military life is luxurious—but neither is living in a crummy apartment and subsisting on a diet of junk food.

While your basic needs are taken care of, you can learn a useful skill. The military has hundreds of jobs that need people to fill them. Virtually everything in civilian life—banks, hospitals, schools, stores—has an equivalent in the armed forces, and the range of positions is wide. The trucks, typewriters, tanks, computers, and ships all require mainte-nance and repair, and someone will teach you how to do it. Best of all, unlike most civilian jobs, occupational specialties in the military require no previous experience. Several jobs are worth a bonus of thousands of dollars just for completing the training. Try to find a deal like that on the outside.

For those with sights on higher education, military service can cut college costs considerably or eliminate them altogether. You can take courses while in uniform, and once you get out you become eligible for veterans' education benefits—even if you've never been in combat. If you've already been to college and want to go to graduate school or even medical school, it's possible to have all your costs taken care of and receive a salary as well.

Even more important than jobs or education, the military can be a place to make fundamental changes in your life. For the young man who has dropped out of school and finds himself on a downward path, the military can provide a place to turn things around. For the young woman who is stuck in a low-skilled, low-paying job with no chance for promotion, the armed forces can give her a chance to move up in the world. And for the person who wants to get away from home and find out what he or she is really capable of, the military can offer an excellent place to begin.

Providing such advantages used to be called "making a man out of you." Those who used this phrase meant that during a hitch in uniform people sometimes changed for the better. They came back more disciplined, able to accept criticism without flying off the handle, and willing to take responsibility for their actions. And, most of all, they came back with a firm grasp of what they wanted to do—no longer the victim of pressures from family or friends. This feature of military service still exists, and for some people can be the best benefit of all.

Whatever good you get out of the armed forces, you are expected to give in return. You surrender control of your life and even of your conscience. The men and women above you will decide and act on what is best for the organization, not necessarily what is best for you. The decisions they make can have a profound effect on your life, and can even end it.

The military is an institution that has no equivalent in civilian life. Those who make it a career often refer to it as a calling. It does not offer great fortune, and it brings fame to only a handful of people. Yet this body of men and women is charged with perhaps the most serious of tasks: defending the country from those who would destroy it. It's not surprising that they call what they do the service. This number-one priority sometimes gets lost in all the talk about jobs and education.

There are other aspects of military life that you'll rarely see in the ads or brochures. The basic purpose of the military is to protect the nation and American interests around the world. Sometimes this means waging wars, and wars mean killing people, who may be innocent civilians, and destroying military and civilian targets. If combat breaks out you will not be asked your opinion of matters. You will be ordered to carry out actions with no hesitation at all, no matter what you think.

The control over your life that is necessary in wartime is present all the time in the military. You lose certain rights that civilians take for granted. Your commanders can order you to perform any task, no matter what you trained for or would rather do. They can move you from base to base and even out of the country. They control your promotions, vacations, appearance, and even the way you talk and act.

And if you don't like it, you can't simply quit.

Making a Decision

Thinking about the armed forces should involve many factors. You need to carefully consider what you want to get out of military life and whether any alternatives might better fit your needs. You should weigh the advantages of the service with the drawbacks that come with putting on a uniform. You need to learn as much about the individual branches as you can.

This book can help you accumulate knowledge about military life in general and individual branches in particular. It is a combination of nuts-and-bolts facts and questions to think about. This book will not make your decision for you; no one book or person can do that. It won't even make a recommendation.

Except one: before you sign papers that commit you to six years of military service, take enough time and learn all you can so that you can make the best decision possible.

2. Questions to Ask Yourself

AFTER THINKING ABOUT IT and talking with a few people, you may begin to think the benefits of military service look pretty appealing. So you walk past a recruiter's booth in a shopping mall or in your high school and pick up some of the brochures.

Before your eyes is spread a feast of educational programs, job training packages, and enlistment options. There are color photographs showing people flying helicopters, operating computers, or scuba diving. You may see a sailor working on an engine as big as a room, or a female mechanic making some technical adjustments on a sleek jet fighter. Or you may simply see people having fun in an exciting place.

These glossy brochures answer all sorts of basic questions about how many jobs are offered, where you can travel, and how long you have to stay in. There are some larger questions, however, that are seldom addressed in this material. An examination of these matters, many of which aren't always apparent to someone outside of the armed forces, can clarify your values and give you some things to think about before joining up.

Here are nine questions to guide your thinking. They are grouped in three areas: the military concept, the military system, and your personality.

The Military Concept

Every war that the United States has fought has been opposed by one group of citizens or another. Some objected to the use of force at all, while others were against a particular conflict. These feelings reached a peak during the Vietnam years, when thousands of people took to the streets and songs of protest reached the Top Forty. Young men began to seriously question whether they could in good conscience take part in the armed forces. It's a question everyone considering military service must think about.

Do I accept the use of force as a tool of national policy? Most people believe the United States should use force to protect its citizens and defend the country. When Adolf Hitler talked about taking over the world, almost everyone saw the need to stop him.

Even when such a threat is less obvious, some policy makers contend we are obligated to oppose it. The war in Vietnam was fought to halt the spread of communism into another country. Recent events in Central America have brought up that subject once more, and, as in Vietnam, the issue is not clear cut.

Going one step further, some strategists contend that the United States is justified in using force to protect American economic and business interests—by maintaining a supply of oil, for example. Does this mean we will fight to keep the Saudi Arabian oil fields open? "Do you want to die for Exxon?" asks one peace group. There is even less agreement here.

As administrations and public opinion change, the emphasis put on the use of force varies. Yet the people in the military must carry out orders from Washington without question.

Can I take part in something I do not support? Obviously if you are against bearing arms you will not spend much time hanging around the recruiter's office. In all the talk about jobs and education, however, it's easy to lose sight of some of the things the military may be called upon to do.

How do you feel about nuclear weapons? Would you be comfortable working in a missile silo or servicing a B-52 that carries nuclear bombs? You might be willing to defend the United States, but how would you feel about fighting against insurgents in Central America? If you served in a National Guard unit, would you have any objection to halting a riot in an American city? Or protecting strikebreakers in a labor dispute?

Outside the military you are free to support whatever cause you want. You can act on your principles by opposing something you do not like, whether your opposition takes the form of discussion or participation in a demonstration.

Inside the military, however, dissent has no place. You are expected to carry out orders and fight where told regardless of your convictions. Are you willing to do this?

The Military System

Steeped in tradition and usually run by the most senior officers, the military often seems a couple of steps behind the society as a whole. Changes do take place, but they are slow in coming. It's worthwhile to examine the way things operate before putting on the uniform.

Can I operate in a large organization? If you are like most eighteen-year-olds, the largest organization you have been a part of is your high school. You may not have been personally aquainted with the principal or headmaster, but at least you knew what he or she looked like.

The military is a vast, sluggish bureaucracy where the chain of command is followed as if it were a lifeline. Sometimes the simplest of requests must pass through a dozen unseen and unknown people, any of whom can turn it down or lay it aside.

It takes special ambition and drive to succeed in this mass of people and paperwork. Some adapt quickly, learning the official and unofficial rules and using them advantageously. Others become frustrated at the system and procedures and seem to be in constant battle with those above them. How would you fit into such an organization?

Can I adapt to the military way of doing things? The armed forces stress uniformity, and they have particular ways of doing some of the most common things. Often the greatest frustrations can come from these small matters.

In the Army's officer candidate school (OCS) men and women are given a diagram showing them exactly where everything on their desk is supposed to go. Included is a paragraph on how handkerchiefs are supposed to be folded inside drawers.

One Air Force officer was told it was unbecoming for an officer to be seen on base carrying a baby. For him this meant that his wife, no matter how tired or uncomfortable she was, had to hold their child as the two walked from place to place.

And in many cases, black men for whom shaving can cause painful ingrown hairs have been forced to keep cleanshaven at all times.

These are small matters, to be sure, but the military insistence on doing things a certain way—no matter what the situation—can prove highly annoying to some people.

Can I adapt to moving around a lot? Seeing new places is one of the attractions of the military, as anyone who has been stationed in Hawaii or Europe can testify. After a while, however, the thrill of picking up and moving is replaced by the hassle of packing possessions, leaving newfound friends, and starting all over again.

The situation is worse if you have a family. It is virtually impossible for the spouse of a military person to have a meaningful job. And it's hard on children to leave their friends and change schools every year.

For the single person, travel can be exciting, but Christmas or another important holiday is no fun when you're sitting in Turkey while the rest of your family is at home eating one.

Your Personality

Some people seem to thrive on military life, while others hate every minute of it. Deciding whether or not to join involves taking a look at yourself and predicting how the partnership will work out.

Do I take orders well? This one is pretty obvious. The person who resists following orders had better start off at the top or stay out altogether.

Officers as well as enlisted personnel may be ordered to perform tasks they don't want to do or work on something that has no apparent usefulness. They may even have to do something in a certain manner when they know another way that would be more efficient.

These orders may come from someone who is younger than you, who has less education or experience, or who you feel is unfit to give orders. Whatever the case, you have to do what you are told; no arguments are allowed.

Can I overlook offensive remarks and attitudes? From the academies on down to boot camp, newcomers to the service face a lot of harassment. Whether from a drill instructor shouting in your face or some lout in the barracks, you are likely to hear derogatory comments about your appearance, sex, race, and any aspect of yourself that draws attention.

Women in the armed forces, particularly enlistees, are likely to have sexual remarks directed at them. These can range from off-color jokes in your presence to outright invitations to engage in sex.

Blacks and other minorities may be subject to racist remarks. For someone who has never let another person get away with such behavior, this can be very difficult to take.

The military is sensitive to charges of sexual and racial harassment, and on an institutional basis it works very hard to prevent it. It cannot, however, prevent individuals, particularly those who hold rank over others, from making sexist or racist comments.

Do I have unrealistic expectations of the armed forces? Sometimes you can get caught up in the power and glory of the ads and get a false impression that military life is going to solve your every problem. Anyone coming in with this attitude is in for a letdown. Many people have made significant changes in their lives while in uniform, and much of the credit can be given to the military experience. But the change has to come from within.

To get a balanced picture of what to expect, you should not only consider what the military offers but what you bring with you. If, for example, you have been fired from your last three jobs, you might do well to consider why this has happened and what you can do to remedy the situation.

As one former Navy chaplain explained, "Some people can go into the military and shape up their lives. But the military will also give you an opportunity to fall flat on your face."

The appropriate question then is: What do I expect from military service, and what can I do to realize my expectations?

What if things don't go as planned? Often people enter the military with a specific goal in mind. A young man may go to the Air Force Academy intending to become a fighter pilot. When he finds he cannot pass aviation training because of severe nausea, he may become despondent. Or a young women enters the Army wanting to become an air traffic controller. She cannot pass a security clearance and is put in a job that involves mostly typing—just the sort of thing she had tried to get away from in civilian life.

Sometimes things do not go as you planned. This may be due to a failing on your part or a situation beyond your control. Although an effort is made to accommodate the wishes of those in uniform, the military is not geared to please the individual. Someone has to guard empty barracks at Fort Campbell, Kentucky; someone has to man the radar station near the Arctic Circle; and someone has to work in the hot engine room of a ship.

You should keep in mind the possibility that nothing will turn out as planned, and that your two or four years on active duty will seem like eight or ten. No one likes this, neither the military authorities or the individuals affected, but it can and does happen.

If you put all of the situations discussed in this chapter together, the military can sound like one awful place. Lots of people, however, come into the service, make it through boot camp with a minimum of hassles, complete the training they wanted, and happily work in the field of their choice. Others find they have to change their plans along the way, and for some the whole thing is plain hell.

In talking with veterans of military service, a phrase one hears again and again is "the proper attitude." Ex-Marine Bob Abernathy puts it best. "Attitude is the whole thing in the military. *You* make what you are in the military."

3. Where Will You Fit In?

I F CONSIDERING WHETHER or not to get into the military is difficult, deciding which branch to join, and in what capacity, is even tougher. Various factors come into play: how much time you wish to put in, what you expect to get out of it, and whether you want an active or a reserve unit.

WHAT DO YOU WANT OUT OF THE SERVICE?

In some respects all the various branches of the armed forces are the same. All of them will get you up at the crack of dawn during basic training, and pay and promotion schedules are roughly similar. Every branch offers job training, and benefits come to all veterans who have been given good discharges.

Despite these similarities there are a great many differences. In the Air Force, for example, the officers are involved in most of the combat while the enlisted people stay on the ground. The Navy offers you a chance to travel all over the world, whereas in the Coast Guard you'll never find yourself spending Christmas in the middle of the Indian Ocean. A soldier in the Army may participate in maneuvers in West Germany, whereas a National Guardsman may assist during flooding or other natural disasters.

Making these decisions forces you to examine why you are getting into the military. For some people this is easy. "From the time I was in the Scouts I wanted to be a pilot," said one Air Force captain. "For me there was no other way to go." Others come from a tradition of serving in a particular branch, and perhaps want to follow in their father's footsteps. For someone coming from a background like this, there's no "which" to decide. For others, an examination of what the military offers is in order.

The Adventure of a Lifetime

For a lot of people the military is just what the ads depict: jets zooming into action off an aircraft carrier, tanks rumbling across a stream, or an elite commando group making its way through a jungle. These people thrive on the excitement the military offers. Patriotism and a desire to serve their country may be a big motivation and acquiring job skills or going to school is secondary.

"I was right out of high school," said one Army officer. "Before long I was a company commander in Vietnam. There I was, a guy in a hole with a radio, orchestrating artillery and air strikes—telling the Navy and the Air Force what to do. The Vietnam experience was the most real thing in my life."

If getting away from home, seeing the world, and doing exciting things appeals to you, then you should head straight for the more action-oriented branches of the military.

Paying for College

Not everyone who considers military service is all that gung-ho about the action and the weaponry. Perhaps the fringe benefits are your primary concern. You may approach the service with a business proposition: I'll give you three years of my life in return for an education.

In recent years military leaders have responded to this concern by developing programs whereby you can set aside money and have the government add to it. In one plan, which requires that you stay in for four years, it is possible to accumulate as much as $25,100, through personal savings and governmental contributions, to pay for college costs. That's enough to put you through most schools in this country.

You can even begin classes while you are in uniform. Provided you meet requirements, the military may pay up to 90 percent of tuition costs while you go to college on your off duty time.

If getting an education is your chief reason for joining the armed forces, there are aspects other than money you should consider. Since you have to save some of the funds yourself, it makes sense to avoid being stationed in an expensive place like Europe. If you want to take classes while in uniform, you should try to get stationed at a place where there are colleges, instead of at a radar outpost in the frozen wastes of Alaska.

Getting a Job

After working as a hamburger flipper or car wash attendant, many young people join up to gain marketable job skills. Every branch offers positions that teach administrative and "people" skills, such as medical records clerk and computer operator.

For more specialized skills, each service varies. If you want to become a diesel mechanic, it stands to reason that the Army, with vast numbers of tanks and trucks, would be the logical choice. Similarly, a person who seeks more technical work might aim for the guidance systems or related fields in the Air Force.

Many people enter the military expecting job training without getting a clear idea of the process. The recruiter can guarantee you the training you want *only* if you meet the qualifications. He or she cannot promise that you will pass the various tests and meet all the conditions for each job.

For example, any job in the armed forces having to do with nuclear materials will require that you pass a security clearance. If you have any history of drug use you are automatically ruled out. The military can even wash you out because you have relatives in a communist country.

If you do not meet the qualifications or if you fail a test, the military is free to put you in a job of its choosing—whether you like it or not.

A general impression given by ads and recruiters is that most military skills are directly transferable to civilian life. This is not always the case. Some positions are similar inside and outside the military, such as court reporter or X-ray specialist. Others have little to do with work on the outside. How many garages do you know that need a field artillery turret mechanic?

Before you sign up for a particular program, make sure you know *all* the qualifications and conditions. This way if your plans have to change then *you* can change them.

The Thing the Ads Never Mention

The ads and posters never show anyone getting wounded or killed. This is the aspect of military service that no one likes to think about, yet it should guide your choice of which branch to join.

If a war—or even a skirmish—breaks out, the forces that take part are likely to suffer casualties. If you are launching your surface-to-air missile, chances are someone is firing at you, too. The war in the Falkland Islands demonstrated that even a country inexperienced in war, such as Argentina, can inflict severe casualties on a militarily superior nation.

Certain air and ground forces, such as the Marines, are traditionally the first ones to enter a fight. If you are in such a group, your chances of coming home wounded—or not coming home at all—are increased.

Few people look forward to armed conflict, but the armed forces are constantly training and preparing for it. If they get into a fight, then so will you. It's worth considering where you want to be when the shooting breaks out.

ACTIVE OR RESERVES?

All of the branches of the service are broken down into two main components—active and reserve. Members of both groups receive the same training, use the same equipment, and are paid at the same rate.

The big difference is how much time they spend in uniform. Active duty is just that—you are on the job full time and are paid full-time wages. In the reserves, you might serve part time or not at all. It depends which reserve you are in.

All officers and enlistees sign up for a commitment of six years. They may be on active duty for anywhere from two through_six years, depending on the branch they enter. However long they stay on active duty, the rest of the six years are spent in the reserves. Some of the time may be spent in the Ready Reserve and some in the Standby Reserve, depending on the enlistment plan. Persons who spend six years on active duty are exempt from reserve duty.

The Ready Reserve is composed of people who train one weekend a month and fifteen days sometime during the year. They are paid for each day spent in uniform. As the name implies, they are ready to be called up in the event of war or some sort of alert.

The Standby Reserve is made up of men and women who have left active duty yet still have some time left on their six-year obligation. They do not have to attend training at all, and they do not get paid. The Standby Reserve can only be called up if Congress declares war or in the event of a national emergency.

The Retired Reserve is staffed by people who have put in enough years to qualify them for retirement benefits. They are paid nothing for being in the Retired Reserve.

This country has always had a reserve force in one form or another. The minutemen of the Revolution were an early version of the Ready Reserve. Various states have had militias that were trained and ready to respond to a call.

The Reserve Officers' Training Corps, or ROTC, was established in the years following World War I to secure a supply of trained officers. When the nation began mobilizing for World War II, the ROTC supplied close to one hundred fifty thousand officers to lead the rapidly swelling armed forces.

The second world war showed that the reserves were prepared to supply plenty of officers, but sadly lacking in enlisted personnel. Congress eventually passed a law requiring those who finished active duty to serve in the reserves. Since then it has become possible to join the reserves and not spend any time on active duty at all, except for the short period of basic and job training.

People who serve in the reserves come at a bargain price for the federal government. The reserves are much less expensive to maintain than the active forces, yet they are there if needed.

They were needed in Korea and Vietnam, and there was a time in the early sixties when international tensions caused President Kennedy to call the reserves into active duty.

Besides being useful to the government, the reserves offer special advantages to members. Some people decide to go straight into the reserves and skip active duty almost entirely. They enlist in a particular branch and go through basic training followed by job training. In both training sessions they are treated just like recruits who are headed for active duty. (Under some programs it is possible to go through basic training one summer and take job training the next summer; this is called the Split Training Option.)

Once the training is over, reservists come home and go to college or get a job or do whatever they want. Their only obligation is to report in uniform to their reserve unit one weekend a month for a two-day drill and to go through a fifteen-day training session sometime during the year. Most units hold these exercises in the summer. They may take place nearby or as far away as Germany or the Far East.

You can think of it as a part-time job. While in uniform— thirty-nine days a year—reservists are paid the same as their active-duty counterparts. At the bottom of the ladder, a private in the Army Reserve would make approximately $900 a year, while a lance corporal, two ranks higher, would make around $1,660 a year.

There are other benefits as well. Many students lower college costs by enrolling in the ROTC program, perhaps winning a scholarship, and enlisted personnel can receive job training in the reserves. Some units offer a $2,000 cash bonus for joining, or $4,000 to be paid over time for educational expenses.

Other incentives include the right to shop at base commissaries and exchanges (grocery and department stores with low prices), inexpensive insurance, and the possibility of overseas trips for training. You can retire after twenty years in the reserves, although you won't start getting checks until you are sixty years old.

The big catch to all this is the possibility of getting called into active service. If that call comes, you have to drop everything and go. Usually this takes place only in wartime, but the reserves have been activated when no war was declared.

Being in the reserves can cause problems at work. Many employers are not thrilled with the two-week training period in the summer. This, plus any vacation you may take, deprives them of your services for a considerable period of time. If you are summoned to active duty, they are required by law to hold your job for you. This is fine for you but of little comfort to your boss.

Reserve duty can also interfere with home life. The weekend drills have an uncanny way of coinciding with birthdays, anniversaries, or other important family activities.

The National Guard

A special reserve force is the National Guard. This will be covered in Chapter 8, but for now the difference is simple: the reserves report to the federal government and are rarely called out for domestic problems. The National Guard reports to the federal *and* the state governments, and can be called out to assist in times of disaster or civil disorder.

OFFICER OR ENLISTED?

Another one of the big choices for someone joining the military is whether to go in as an officer or as an enlisted person. At first the choice might seem obvious—go in as an officer. You make more money and there are fewer people to tell you what to do.

It's actually more complex than that. Once more you have to consider what you expect out of the service. Do you plan to make it a career? Or are you using the military as a means of learning a job skill or getting money for college? Your answers to these questions will determine the path you should take.

Although each branch of the service does things differently, there are some things about officers and enlisted personnel that are the same across the board.

Officers. An officer in the military is the equivalent of a corporate manager in civilian life. Over 90 percent of officers have completed four years of college, and their pay is approximately double that of enlisted personnel.

Besides the obvious benefit of command, officers are generally the only ones who can take aviation training. They may also get sent back to college for an advanced degree or spend time in the civilian sector learning managerial skills.

After being commissioned, officers have a certain number of years they have to serve. After that they can resign unless they have lengthened their obligation by taking flight training or any other special educational program.

Enlisted. An enlisted person in the military is equivalent to an hourly worker or a supervisor in the civilian world. The various branches have different names for the ranks, so to simplify things they are often referred to by numbers. An E-1 is the lowest rank; someone holding it would be called a private in the Army and the Marine Corps, an airman basic in the Air

Force, and a seaman recruit in the Navy. Enlisted ranks go as high as E-9.

The first two or three promotions are more or less automatic, provided you progress satisfactorily. Although each branch of the service does things differently, you generally advance from E-1 to E-2 at the end of six months, and to E-3 at the end of a year. E-4 will take anywhere from one and a half to two and a half years. From there on up promotion is based on your performance on the job, on tests, on your commanding officer's recommendation, and on the needs of your particular branch.

Not everyone starts out at E-1. If you have a particular skill the service needs or have completed some college courses, you can sometimes enter at E-2 or E-3. In times of combat people often rise in rank much more quickly than normally.

Your pay is based on your rank, how long you have been in, and the situations in which you are serving. Special pay is given, for example, to those on sea duty or hazardous duty.

In addition to the pay, the services provide food, uniforms, and housing for enlisted personnel. If any of these are not available, you will be paid a nontaxable allowance so you can provide these items yourself. For example, an enlisted man who is a recruiter may not work near a military dining hall. In this case he is eligible for a food allowance. Similarly, a female sergeant who works at a small military installation where there are no barracks for women may draw a housing allowance so she can rent an apartment. If you have dependents the allowances are higher.

Let's focus on the Navy to get an idea of pay. If you become a seaman recruit (E-1), you will receive $573.60 per month. After six months you will be promoted to seaman apprentice (E-2) and get $642.90 per month. Whenever you make seaman (E-3), your pay goes up to $668.40 a month—$704.70 if you've been in more than two years. If you stay in the Navy and become a master chief petty officer (E-9), after twenty-six years you will make a minimum of $2,215.20 per month. And this doesn't include the various allowances.

Getting an Education

Many people look at the military as their ticket to higher education. It can serve that purpose for both officers and enlisted persons, though in differing fashions.

The armed forces, through the ROTC, will help pay for your college education before you begin active duty. You can thus go through college at the same time as other people your age and enter military service about the time your friends are getting their first jobs.

For an enlisted person it is possible to take courses while in uniform, but the bulk of your college education will have to wait until you finish your active duty. After four years of service, under special programs, it is possible to come up with as much as $25,100 for college. You will, however, find yourself in classes with people who are three or four years younger than you. This may be socially inconvenient or it may not bother you at all, but it is something to consider. Once you graduate, you can enter the job of your choice with no military obligation hanging over you.

Advancement

Both officer and enlisted ranks have advantages and disadvantages. The one thing they share is the opportunity to advance. Unskilled high school dropouts can enter the enlisted ranks and, with a lot of work, elevate themselves to a position that commands a lot of respect.

Similarly, a young person can come into the officer corps as a second lieutenant and work hard, taking the breaks where they come, and wind up with a major command.

It's even possible to work from enlisted to officer status through the various officer candidate programs. You can literally go from servicing a jet fighter to flying it if you work hard and meet all the qualifications.

Promotion to the higher ranks is not automatic. Some people get fed up and leave, viewing the military as a sluggish bureaucracy or a heartless machine. The opportunity is there, however, for ambitious men and women to come in and carve out a career filled with advancement and honor. It's up to you.

Jobs and Career Preparation

If you are entering the military to learn a specific skill, then you go in as an enlisted person. Your active duty commitment will probably be three or four years; then you can return to the civilian life and begin earning money with your trade. You may have a reserve commitment to honor for two or three years, but for the most part you are a civilian once more.

The managerial experience an officer gets is as varied as the branches of the service. You learn to function in a large organization and work with a diverse group of people under unusual circumstances. Keep in mind, though, that managing people who have to follow orders and who cannot quit is considerably different from managing people in the civilian world.

ABOUT THOSE JOBS

When you spread out the brochures from all of the services it looks as if you have hundreds of jobs to choose from, all with pictures of men and women who seem to be enjoying themselves immensely.

In practice, however, the list you will choose from will be much shorter. Your abilities, sex, the needs of the service, and the length of time you plan to stay will all reduce the hundreds of possibilities to a more manageable number. And no matter which branch of the service you approach, you'll go through the same procedure to determine the job for you.

First of all—even before joining—you take the Armed Services Vocational Aptitude Battery exam (ASVAB). This test is often given in high schools, but if you haven't had it your recruiter will send you to a testing center where you will take the exam and receive a physical on the same day.

If you have no skills, the ASVAB gives the recruiters a good idea of where your talents lie. Many people are surprised when the test results show nothing in common with their interests, and some are disappointed when told they have little aptitude in the field they like. Others find to their delight that they are rated high in the very thing they want to do.

Certain jobs in the armed forces require high scores on the ASVAB. If your score is not that high, then you cannot apply to be trained for one of those jobs. Others require excellent vision or some other physical standard that you have to meet. Whatever the case, your scores and physical condition will shorten the list of possible jobs.

If you already have a skill and want to use it, you might be able to enter the military at a higher rank and be eligible for accelerated promotion. You still have to go through basic training, but you get paid more for doing so.

If you are female, federal law prohibits you from having a combat job or any position that would require you to be in a combat zone. You cannot, for example, fly an attack helicopter or drive a tank. Certain jobs requiring heavy exertion are not available to women.

The number of years you plan to stay on active duty enters into all this, too. Some jobs require extensive training and are not available for some of the shorter enlistment periods. This further trims down the list of possibilities.

Taking all these matters into account, you and a *classifier*, a special employee in an induction center, sit down and come up with the group of jobs from which you can choose. Let's say you decide you want to become an industrial welder in the Army. Now you need to see if the Army needs an industrial welder. The classifier checks the computer and learns that an opening for a welder will come up in ten months. Under the delayed entry plan, you can join now and actually enter the Army several months later, taking basic training and welding training just in time to be ready when the opening occurs.

That's how it is supposed to work. But if the Army has plenty of industrial welders you'll have to choose again. You keep going down the list until you and the Army find a job that fits.

You can get a cash bonus for selecting one of a certain list of jobs. Some of the more technical ones require long training periods—maybe as long as a year—and the military uses the bonus to make all this schooling worthwhile. Other jobs are combat-related and have little equivalent in the civilian world. A $5,000 bonus can suddenly make these positions much more attractive.

Finally you are ready to make your choice. Your ASVAB scores fit the job, the military needs someone to fill it, and it is offered for persons staying in the amount of time you are. The recruiter congratulates you on your choice and guarantees you'll get the training.

But he won't guarantee you'll get the job. The military seeks to put people where planned, but if it turns out that you are needed somewhere else it'll put you there. Sometimes this is only temporary, and occasionally you will like the second job even more, but quite a few people find themselves doing something other than what they want. Keep that in mind.

THE BRANCHES OF THE MILITARY

Trying to describe each branch of the armed forces in just a few pages is akin to relating the history of the country in a ninety-minute television special. It can be done, but a lot has to be condensed. So it is in the following chapters on the Army, Navy, Air Force, Marines, National Guard, and the Coast Guard.

The military organizations in this country are constantly reacting to changes in world situations and national politics. New weapon systems and new ways of doing things are evolving all the time. The switch from a draft to an all-volunteer force has been one of the biggest changes.

With the increased dependence on recruiting, programs to meet particular needs are constantly being considered as well as new ways to bring in qualified men and women. Unsuccessful policies are replaced by new ones. If the new ones work, they are adopted by other branches of the service and further refined.

All this is a manner of saying that this book is only a guide to what the military is like and what it can offer you. From these pages you can get a general sense of each branch and its attractions, but you'll have to check with a recruiter to find out the up-to-the-minute offerings.

And for the best information on what each branch is like, talk to someone who is in it now or who has just gotten out. There's nothing like hearing it from someone who's been there.

4. The Army

WITH 781,700 MEN AND WOMEN on active duty, the Army is the nation's largest fighting force. Troops are stationed in this country and in Europe, Korea, and Panama.

History

The Continental Army was established in 1775 with George Washington in command. After the revolutionary war the country turned to other matters, and when the War of 1812 came along the Army was ill prepared. The development of the U.S. Military Academy at West Point and greater attention from Congress fostered an Army that handled itself well in the Mexican War of the 1840s.

The Civil War, in which the officers of the Army led troops against each other, proved what a deadly force the Army had become. The strategy and tactics perfected in the 1860s conflict, particularly the use of the railroads and the telegraph, served as a pattern for future wars around the world.

The needs of World War I swelled the Army to over 4 million men, and the height of World War II saw over 11 million men in uniform.

The Army fought communist forces for the first time in the Korean Conflict, eventually securing the border of what is now South Korea.

The 1960s saw the Army in Vietnam, in a conflict that bitterly divided America and became one of the greatest frustrations in the history of the Army. North Vietnamese forces proved elusive in the jungles of Vietnam despite large numbers of U.S. troops and the use of ultramodern combat hardware.

Since Vietnam the Army has undergone a period of self-examination, and changes have been made. The biggest has been the end of the draft, in 1973. The switch to all-volunteer forces has brought many new features to the Army. Vocational and educational opportunities have been emphasized, and more opportunities have opened for women.

Length of Hitch

Officers. All commissioned officers have to serve the Army for six years, splitting their obligation between active and reserve duty. It breaks down like this, in years:

	Active Duty	Ready Reserve	Standby Reserve*
ACTIVE ARMY			
U.S. Military Academy	5	0	1
ROTC with scholarship	4	0	2
ROTC without scholarship	3	0	3
Officer candidate school	3	0	3
ARMY RESERVE			
Reserve Forces Duty	¼ – ½	remainder of 6	

*Officers can stay in the Ready Reserve if they prefer.

The time you spend on active duty pays the Army for your schooling. If you want to take further training the Army is willing—but you have to stay longer.

Here are some of the things that can add to your obligation:

☐ *Graduate school.* If the Army sends you to graduate school you must stay in uniform two years for every one year in school.

☐ *Promotion.* If you accept a promotion you obligate yourself for another two years.

☐ *Aviation training.* Although the Army is not the Air Force, it has over eighty-five hundred aircraft, mostly helicopters. Flight training for helicopter duty lasts approximately nine months, and aviators must serve four years after completing flight school.

An important note: An officer's extra obligations can be served simultaneously. This means that, if you go through Army ROTC and then take flight training, you will not owe the Army eight years. If you entered flight training right after commissioning, you would probably only be obligated to serve five years.

Enlisted. Those who enlist in the Army commit themselves to six years of service in a combination of active and reserve duty. Those who join the Army Reserve spend only a few months on active duty before going into Ready Reserve.

The Army offers tours of two to four years active duty. The two-year hitch is the shortest of all the services.

Here is a breakdown of the enlistment programs by years:

	Active Duty	Ready Reserve	Standby Reserve
Regular Army	2	0	4
	3	0	3
	4	0	2
Army Reserve	1/3 – 2/3	6	0

Basic Training

"Going through basic" is perhaps the most feared and the most bragged-about experience in the Army this side of combat. Forty to fifty recruits form a platoon and are trained by a noncommissioned officer known as the drill instructor.

Despite electronic vision enhancers, personnel sensors, and other high-tech hardware, the Army is first and foremost a ground force. When you take basic training you can expect around a hundred miles of marching—day and night—camping, camouflage, and plenty of time on the rifle range. It all lasts for seven weeks.

A Typical Day. Here is an hour-by-hour schedule for a day in the sixth week of basic training. This is perhaps the toughest day you'll have, for instead of hitting the sack at night, you'll hit the road for a night march and bivouac.

4:30 A.M.	First call
4:45–5:30	Physical training
5:30–6:00	Decided by drill instructor
6:00–6:30	Breakfast
6:30–7:00	Inspection
7:00–9:50	U.S. weapons familiarization
9:50–12:00 P.M.	Concealment and maneuvers
12:00–1:00	Lunch
1:00–4:00	Hand grenade assault course
4:00–5:00	Dinner
5:00–6:00	Personal time
7:00–Completion	Evening activities
12:00 A.M.	March and bivouac

In the training sessions you will learn how the Army operates and how you are expected to operate in combat. Topics covered include such things as:

First aid	Military customs and courtesies
M-16 familiarization	Camouflage
Grenade training	Gas mask training
Close-order drill	Hygiene and sanitation
Promotion	Uniform Code of Military Justice

Location. Army basic training takes place at the following forts. Men can train at any of the seven installations, but women are trained only at the first four. Except for variations to allow for physical differences, women receive the same training as men.

Installation	Nearest City
Fort Dix	Trenton, New Jersey
Fort Jackson	Columbia, South Carolina
Fort Leonard Wood	Rolla, Missouri
Fort McClellan	Anniston, Alabama
Fort Bliss	El Paso, Texas
Fort Knox	Louisville, Kentucky
Fort Sill	Lawton, Oklahoma

Jobs

The Army offers more job categories than any other branch of the service. They call them Military Occupational Specialties, or MOS's for short, and there are over three hundred from which to choose. They range from small weapons repairer to club manager, from radio/TV broadcasting production coordinator to tank turret mechanic.

Women are barred from combat jobs such as driving tanks, although they can serve in combat-support specialties as truck drivers, medics, and so on. The Army estimates that 17 percent of the MOS's are barred to women, yet this figure can be misleading. Infantryman, for example, is just one of the titles on the list, yet this job is held by thousands of men.

The job of infantryman obviously involves combat, yet women are barred from some specialties that at first do not seem combat-related. Chief among these are the building trades, such as plumbing, interior electrical work, and the operation of heavy construction equipment. In 1982 the Army began screening women to test their physical abilities before allowing them to choose jobs that require great muscular strength.

The ASVAB has a big influence on the number of MOS possibilities open to you. Once you decide what you want, the

Army will guarantee you the training, and in some situations it will guarantee your first base of assignment—if a job is open for you there. That can be a big if.

Job training, called Advanced Individual Training (AIT), can last anywhere from a few weeks to almost a year. Here are three career fields and a sampling of the jobs offered in each.

☐ *Air defense artillery.* A person in this MOS area will emplace, assemble, test, maintain, and fire air defense weapons systems. Related tasks include operating fire control equipment, radar, computers, automatic data transmission systems, and associated power-supply equipment. The training focuses on acquiring basic mechanical and electrical knowledge.

This MOS area includes combat jobs that are barred to women.

☐ *Finance and accounting.* An organization as large as the Army offers thousands of opportunities to use these job skills. Persons in this field maintain pay records of military personnel, prepare vouchers for payment, prepare reports, and disburse funds. They perform tasks such as budgeting, allocating, auditing, and compiling and analyzing statistical data.

☐ *Transportation.* Persons in this MOS area drive and maintain passenger vehicles and light, medium, and heavy cargo vehicles. They may pilot small boats or even perform as air traffic controllers.

Advanced Training

Recruits who have enlisted for a longer period of active duty find advanced training programs available to them. One of these is the Army Apprenticeship Program, which enables you to earn a certificate from the U.S. Department of Labor that is recognized by civilian employers. It states that you have achieved journeyworker status and are skilled at your particular trade.

After you receive the training you log your work hours in a special book. Depending on the trade you choose, you have to log between two thousand and eight thousand hours to get your certificate. You can do so, however, only if the Army assigns you to work in your chosen field, which it tries to do. But sometimes the Army needs you elsewhere, and you will not have time during your enlistment to complete the log. You can always reenlist, but that's another story.

Here are some of the trades that come under the Army Apprenticeship Program:

Plant equipment operator
Engineering surveyor
Hydraulic equipment
  repairer
Automobile mechanic
Cook
Still photographer

Architectural drafter
Photograph interpreter
Industrial welder
Automobile body repairer
Radio/TV repairer
TV cable installer

Bonuses

Since Army recruits have their choice of training, sometimes there is a shortage of people in a particular job. Often those jobs are combat-related and have little equivalent in civilian life. Other times the jobs require extensive schooling. To fill these jobs the Army offers cash, payable when you complete the necessary training. Once the MOS attracts enough people the offer is withdrawn.

For that reason it is impossible to list the jobs that rate bonuses right now. For such a list you need to check with your Army recruiter. Jobs for which bonuses have been given in the past include:

Air traffic control operator $5,000
Voice intercept identifier   4,000
Foreign language–related jobs   3,000

Job List

Following is the Army's list of MOS's. Those that are barred to women are marked with an asterisk.

Accounting specialist
ADA operations and intelligence
assistant
*ADA short range gunnery crewman
*ADA short range missile crewman
Administrative specialist
ADMSE repairer
ADP maintenance supervisor
*Aerial electronic warning defense
equipment repairer
Aerial sensor specialist
Aerial sensor specialist (OV-ID)
Aerial surveillance infrared
repairer (Reserves only)
Aerial surveillance photographic
equipment repairer (Reserve)
Aerial surveillance radar repairer
(Reserves only)
Aerial surveillance sensor repairer
Airbrake repairer (Reserves only)
Aircraft components repair
supervisor
Aircraft electrician
Aircraft fire control repairer
Aircraft maintenance senior
sergeant
Aircraft pneudraulics repairer
Aircraft powerplant repairer
Aircraft powertrain repairer
Aircraft quality control supervisor
Aircraft structural repairer
Aircraft weapon systems repairer
Air defense artillery senior sergeant
Air defense radar repairer
Airplane repairer
Air traffic control (ATC) tower
operator
Ammunition foreman
Ammunition inspector
Ammunition specialist
Animal care specialist
Antenna installer specialist
AN/TSQ-73 air defense
Artillery command and control
system operator/repairer
Area intelligence specialist

Armament/fire control
maintenance supervisor
*Armor senior sergeant
Artillery repairer
ATC radar controller
*Atomic demolition munitions
specialist
Attack helicopter repairer
Audio/TV specialist
Audio-visual equipment repairer
Automatic data
telecommunications center
operator
AVIONIC communications
equipment repairer
AVIONIC equipment
maintenance supervisor
AVIONIC mechanic
AVIONIC navigation and flight
control equipment repairer
AVIONIC special equipment
repairer
Ballistic/land combat/light air
defense systems maintenance
chief
Baritone or euphonium player
Bassoon player
Behavioral science specialist
Biological sciences assistant
Biomedical equipment specialist,
advanced
Biomedical equipment specialist,
basic
Brass group leader
*Bridge crewmember
Broadcast journalist
Cable splicer
Calibration specialist
*Cannon crewman
*Cannon fire direction specialist
Cannon/missile senior sergeant
Card and tape writer (Reserve)
Cardiac specialist
*Carpentry and masonry specialist
Cartographer
*Cavalry scout

Central office operations operator
Chapel activities specialist
CHAPPARRAL/REDEYE
  repairer
*CHAPPARRAL system mechanic
Chemical laboratory specialist
Chemical senior sergeant
Clarinet player
Club manager
Combat area surveillance radar
  repairer
*Combat engineer
*Combat engineering senior
  sergeant
Combat telecommunications
  center operator
Communications-electronics
  maintenance chief
Communications-electronics
  operations chief
Computer/machine operator
*Concrete and asphalt equipment
  operator
Construction engineering
  supervisor
Construction equipment repairer
Construction equipment
  supervisor
*Construction surveyor
Cornet or trumpet player
Correctional specialist
Counterintelligence agent
Court reporter
DAS 3 computer repairer
Data processing NCO
*Defense acquisition radar operator
Defense acquisition radar mechanic
Dental laboratory specialist
Dental specialist
Dial/manual central office repairer
*Diver
DSTE repairer
Electronic instrument repairer
Electronic switching systems
  repairer
*Engineer track vehicle crewman

Enlisted bandleader
ENT specialist
Environmental health specialist
Equal opportunity NCO
Equipment records and parts
  specialist
EW/Intercept systems repairer
EW/SIGINT analyst
EW/SIGINT chief
EW/SIGINT emitter identifier
  locator
EW/SIGINT morse interceptor
EW/SIGINT non-communications
  interceptor
EW/SIGINT non-morse
  interceptor
EW/SIGINT voice interceptor
Explosive ordnance disposal
  specialist
Eye specialist
Fabric repair specialist
Field artillery computer repairer
*Field artillery firefinder radar
  operator
Field artillery meteorological
  crewmember
*Field artillery radar crewmember
*Field artillery surveyor
Field artillery target acquisition
  senior sergeant
*Field artillery target acquisition
  specialist
Field artillery turret mechanic
Field general COMSEC repairer
Field radio repairer
Field systems COMSEC repairer
Finance senior sergeant
Finance specialist
Fire control instrument repairer
*Fire control systems repairer
Firefighter
Fire support specialist
Fixed ciphony repairer
Fixed cryptographic equipment
  repairer
Fixed station radio repairer

Flight operations coordinator
Flute or piccolo player
Food service specialist
Forward area alerting radar
  repairer
French horn player
Fuel and electrical systems
  repairer
FV infantryman
*General construction equipment
  operator
General engineering supervisor
Graves registration specialist
Ground control approach radar
  repairer
*Ground surveillance radar
  crewman
Guitar player
HAWK fire control crewmember
HAWK missile crewmember
*Heavy antiarmor weapons
  crewmember
*Heavy construction equipment
  operator
Heavy lift helicopter repairer
Heavy wheel vehicle mechanic
HERCULES electronics
  mechanic
HERCULES fire control
  crewmember
HERCULES missile
  crewmember
Hospital food service specialist
IBM 360 repairer
Illustrator
Image interpreter
Improved HAWK continuous
  wave radar repairer
Improved HAWK fire control
  mechanic
Improved HAWK fire control
  repairer
Improved HAWK firing section
  mechanic
Improved HAWK information
  coordination central mechanic

Improved HAWK
  launcher/mechanical systems
  repairer
Improved HAWK maintenance
  chief
Improved HAWK master
  mechanic
Improved HAWK pulse radar
  repairer
Improved TOW vehicle/infantry
  fighting vehicle/cavalry fighting
  vehicle system mechanic
Improved TOW vehicle/infantry
  fighting vehicle/cavalry fighting
  vehicle turret mechanic
*Indirect fire infantryman
Industrial gas production specialist
  (Reserve)
*Infantryman
Intelligence analyst
Intelligence senior sergeant
*Interior electrician
Interrogator
Journalist
LANCE crewmember/MLRS
  sergeant
Land combat support system test
  specialist/LANCE
Repairer
Laundry and bath specialist
Legal clerk
Lifting and loading equipment
  operator
*Light air defense artillery
  crewmember (Reserve)
Light wheel vehicle/power
  generation repairer
Locomotive electrician (Reserves
  only)
Locomotive operator (Reserves
  only)
Locomotive repairer (Reserves
  only)
Machinist
MANSPADS crewman (man
  portable air defense system)

Marine hull repairer
Marine senior sergeant
Material storage and handling
   specialist
Material control and accounting
   specialist
Materials quality specialist
Mechanical maintenance
   supervisor
Medical laboratory specialist
Medical specialist
Medical supply specialist
*Medium helicopter repairer
Metal worker
Meteorological observer
*MI armor crewman
Military police
MLRS/LANCE operation fire
   direction specialist
Motion picture specialist
Motor transport operator
Multichannel communications
   equipment operator
Multiple launch rocket system
   crewmember
*M48-M60A1/A3 armor
   crewmember
M60A1/A3 tank systems mechanic
M60A1/A3 tank turret mechanic
M60A2 tank system mechanic
M60A2 tank turret mechanic
*Nuclear/biological/chemical
   specialist
NCR 500 computer repairer
NIKE-HERCULES fire control
   mechanic
NIKE-HERCULES
   missile-launcher repairer
*NIKE high power radar-simulator
   repairer
NIKE maintenance chief
NIKE test equipment repairer
NIKE track radar repairer
Nuclear medicine specialist
Nuclear weapons electronics
   specialist
Nuclear weapons maintenance
   specialist
Oboe player
Observation airplane repairer
Observation/scout helicopter
   repairer
Occupational therapy specialist
Office machine repairer
Operating room specialist
Operations central repairer
Optical laboratory specialist
Orthopedic specialist
Orthotic specialist
Parachute rigger
Patient administration specialist
Patient care specialist
PATRIOT missile crewmember
PATRIOT missile mechanic
Percussion group leader
Percussion player
PERSHING electrical-mechanical
   repairer
PERSHING electronics material
   specialist
PERSHING electronics repairer
PERSHING missile crewmember
Personnel actions specialist
Personnel administration specialist
Personnel management specialist
Personnel records specialist
Personnel senior sergeant
Petroleum laboratory specialist
Petroleum supply specialist
Pharmacy specialist
Photo and layout specialist
Photolithographer
Physical activities specialist
Physical therapy specialist
Piano player
*Plumber
Power generation equipment
   repairer
Prime power production specialist
Programmer/analyst
Psychiatric specialist
Public affairs/audio-visual chief

Punch card machine repairer
*Quarrying specialist
Quartermaster and chemical
  equipment repairer
Radio operator
Radio teletype operator
Radio/television systems specialist
Railway car repairer (reserves only)
Railway movement coordinator
  (Reserves only)
Railway section repairer (Reserves
  only)
Railway senior sergeant
Recruiter
Reenlistment NCO
Respiratory specialist
Satellite communications ground
  station equipment repairer
Saxophone player
Self-propelled field artillery system
  mechanic
Senior supply sergeant
SHILLELAGH repairer

SIGSEC analyst
Small arms repairer
*Smoke operations specialist
Special agent
Special bandperson
Special electronic devices repairer
Station technical controller
Stenographer
Still photographic specialist
Strategic microwave systems
  repairer
Strategic satellite/microwave
  systems operator
Structures specialist
Subsistence supply specialist
TACFIRE operations specialist
Tactical circuit controller
Tactical communications systems
  operator/mechanic
Tactical microwave systems
  repairer
Tactical satellite/microwave
  systems operator

*Tactical transport helicopter
  repairer
Tactical wire operations specialist
Tank turret repairer
Technical drafting specialist
Technical engineering supervisor
Teletypewriter repairer
Terminal operations coordinator
Topographic engineering
  supervisor
Topographic instrument repair
  specialist
Topographic surveyor
TOW/DRAGON repairer
Track vehicle mechanic
Track vehicle repairer
Traffic management coordinator
Train crewmember (Reserves only)
*Transmission and distribution
  specialist
Transportation senior sergeant
Trombone player

Tuba player
TV/radio broadcast operations chief
*Unattended ground sensor
  specialist
Unit/supply specialist
UNIVAC 1004/1005 DCT 9000
  system repairer
Utilities equipment repairer
Utility-helicopter repairer
Veterinary specialist
*VULCAN system mechanic
VULCAN repairer
Watercraft engineer
Watercraft operator
Water treatment and plumbing
  systems specialist
Weapons support radar repairer
Wheel vehicle repairer
Wire systems installer/operator
Woodwind group leader
XM-1 tank system mechanic
XM-1 tank turret mechanic
X-Ray specialist

5. The Navy

FOR OVER TWO HUNDRED YEARS the Navy has been the chief means of projecting U.S. military might around the world. From the wooden ships of colonial times to the present-day Trident submarines, the U.S. Navy has accumulated a record of victories unmatched by any other country.

Navy sailors go out to sea in over four hundred fifty combat ships and more than six thousand aircraft. This fighting force is staffed by five hundred forty-eight thousand men and women on active duty.

History

The Navy was officially established in 1798, but its celebrated birthday is Ocober 13, 1775, when the Second Continental Congress authorized the purchase of two vessels. That fledgling Navy is best remembered by a quote from John Paul Jones, captain of the *Bonhomme Richard*. In the thick of a ready to give up. Jones retorted, "I have not yet begun to fight!" This spirit set the tone for future naval battles.

The Navy protected the young United States, and most of its battles were fought to keep the vital sea lanes open. In its most far reaching move, the Navy carried out a daring raid on a group of Barbary pirates in the Mediterranean Sea.

The Civil War brought forth another famous Navy quote, this time from David Farragut as he told his crew to disregard the mines in the Mobile harbor. "Damn the torpedoes! Full steam ahead!" he thundered. Farragut was not a man to waste words.

Wooden ships gave way to steel ones, and in 1898 the United States surprised Spain and won a victory under Admiral Dewey in the Philippine Islands.

In World War I the Navy ferried millions of men and tons of materiel to Europe and for the first time waged extensive antisubmarine warfare. World War II began for the United States with a devastating attack by the Japanese on Pearl Harbor, Hawaii. Much of the Pacific fleet was sunk in that bold move, and a Japanese admiral was said to have remarked, "I fear we have awakened a sleeping giant." His words proved prophetic.

Although the Korean and Vietnamese conflicts included none of the epic sea battles of World War II, the Navy used battleships to bombard positions far inland, and Navy fliers flew extensive missions over battle areas. In Vietnam the Navy patrolled the rivers and supported the Marines on land.

In recent years the Navy has concentrated on moderniz-ing the fleet and building a new generation of submarines. The missiles carried by these silent ships constitute one-third of the nation's nuclear defense system.

Length of Hitch

Officers. All commissioned officers are obligated to serve in the Navy for six years—four or five years on active duty, and the reminder in either the Ready Reserve or the Standby Reserve.

The obligation breaks down like this, in years:

	Active Duty	Ready or Standby Reserve
U.S. Naval Academy	5	1
Naval ROTC	4	2
Officer candidate school	4	2

Your four or five years of service more or less pay back the Navy for the schooling you have received. If you take additional training—if the Navy invests even more in you—then your obligation increases accordingly.

Here are some things that can add to your obligation:

☐ *Graduate school.* If the Navy pays for your graduate schooling you must stay in uniform one year for every year of school you attend. If the Navy sends you to medical school the same rule applies, but you begin working off the obligation after internship and residency.

☐ *Promotion.* Getting promoted during your initial obligation period does not mean you'll have to serve longer. Once you reach the rank of lieutenant commander, however, you owe the Navy three years whenever you accept a higher rank.

☐ *Aviation training.* Flight training is perhaps the most expensive schooling in the Navy, and for that reason the obligation is the longest. If you become a flight officer, such as a navigator, bombardier, or an electronics officer, you must serve four years after completing flight school. The training averages a year in length.

If you decide to become a Navy pilot, then you can add six and a half years to your obligation. Pilot training takes one and a half years, and then you owe the Navy five more years.

An important note: Not all of these add-ons are cumulative. For instance, if you were to go through Naval ROTC and then take pilot training you would not owe the Navy ten and a half years. If you were to go into flight training right after you were commissioned you would have to serve the Navy only six and a half years.

Enlisted. Everyone who enlists in the Navy signs up for a six-year hitch. How that six years is spent, however, depends on the enlistment plan you choose.

If you join the Naval Reserve, you need spend only a minimal amount of time on active duty—usually just enough to cover basic training and job training.

Those who opt for the active Navy must spend three to six years on active duty, and the remainder of the six years in the reserve. If you sign up for six years of active duty you have no obligation to serve in the reserve.

As with officers, the amount of training an enlisted person takes may affect the length of active duty. For example, if you were to select the Advanced Electronics Field Training you would have to sign up for six years.

Why? In advanced electronics or a similar field, your training will take almost two years to complete. If you signed up for only three years then the Navy would get only one year of work from you before you would be eligible to leave. As elsewhere in the military, the more the Navy invests in you the longer they expect you to stay.

Here are the options, in years:

	Active Duty	Ready Reserve	Standby Reserve*
ACTIVE NAVY	3	2	1
	4	0	2
	5	0	1
	6	0	0
NAVAL RESERVE			
Active Mariner Program	3	2	1
Active Mariner Apprenticeship Training Program	3	2	1
Training and Administration of the Reserves Program	4	0	2
Ready Mariner Program	½–1½	remainder of 6	0

*You can serve in the Ready Reserve instead, if you prefer.

Basic Training

Groups of approximately eighty recruits make up a company, which is under the watchful eye of the company commander, the equivalent of an Army drill instructor. He or she leads the company through the seven-week training period.

One of the first things a recruit learns is the way the Navy talks. The Navy is very proud of its seafaring traditions, and many of the terms used on land and water come from the days of wooden ships. A bathroom is called a head. The hospital or clinic is called a sick bay, and the kitchen is a galley. The drinking fountain is a scuttlebutt, and candy or gum is called gedunk.

A typical day. Basic training in the Navy incorporates intensive mental and physical activities. Your day might shape up like this.

4:30 A.M.	Reveille
5:10–5:50	Physical training
6:00–7:20	Barracks cleanup and breakfast
7:30–8:10	Decided by company commander
8:20–9:00	Training period 1
9:10–9:50	Training period 2
10:00–10:40	Training period 3
10:50–11:30	Training period 4
11:40–12:20 P.M.	Training period 5[1]
12:30–1:10	Training period 6[1]
1:20–2:00	Training period 7
2:10–2:50	Training period 8
3:00–3:40	Training period 9
3:50–4:30	Training period 10
4:40–5:20	Training period 11
5:30–6:00	Evening meal
6:00–7:30	Shower, shave, and shine shoes
7:30–8:15	All hands on cleaning stations; clean barracks

---

1. One of these is the lunch period.

8:15–9:25	Recruit instructions—term, rank, knot of the day, etc.—and night bunk check
9:25–9:30	Tattoo (preparation for taps)
9:30	Taps

The training periods will find you learning about life on ship and such things as Navy promotions and policies and military drill. Other topics include:

Accident prevention   Basic deck seamanship
Chain of command   Cultural adjustments
Damage control   Firefighting
Hand salutes and   History of the Navy
  greetings   Officer recognition
Navy mission and   Survival at sea
  organization   Uniform Code of Military
Personal hygiene   Justice
Watchstanding

The physical part. Physical training is held every day, and there are even remedial physical workouts for people who are having a difficult time. A recruit is tested four times during basic training; here are some of the requirements for the final men's test:

Exercise	Amount Required
Pushups (hands under chin)	20
Situps (six-count situp)	15
Jumping jacks	75
Running	2¼ mi. in 18 min.

As might be expected, the Navy teaches its people to swim. You must be able to:

☐ Enter the water feet first from a height of five feet and float or tread water for five minutes;
☐ Enter the water in the deep end of a pool and swim fifty yards, using any stroke, keeping the head above the water; and
☐ Put on and care for the inherently buoyant and the CO_2-inflatable life jackets.

Location. Men undergo basic training at Great Lakes, Illinois; Orlando, Florida; or San Diego, California. Women undergo basic only in Orlando.

Jobs

The Navy offers approximately ninety job categories, ranging from chaplain's assistant to aviation antisubmarine warfare operator. Jobs are called *ratings* in the Navy. As in most of the other branches of the service, to be eligible for the more advanced ratings you have to plan to stay in longer.

The needs of the Navy and your ASVAB scores determine which job ratings you quality for. Those two, plus the amount of time you decide to stay, will determine the ratings from which you can choose.

It's a rare person in the Navy who never serves on a ship, and this poses problems for women, who are forbidden by law from serving on combat vessels. They can ship out for brief periods when a vessel does not have a combat assignment, and they can serve anytime on auxiliary or noncombat ships, but the noncombat restrictions severely limit the number of jobs available to women. The Department of Defense estimates that 14 percent of the Navy ratings are barred to women.

Once a rating is selected, the Navy guarantees the recruit the training that he or she signs up for. After basic training the sailor goes to "A" school to learn the skill. "A" schools are all over the country—some quite far from the sea—and the length of schooling ranges from six weeks to more than forty weeks.

Here are three ratings and the length of training required:

☐ *Lithographer.* A lithographer works in a print shop

turning out magazines, brochures, newspapers, training manuals, and any other printed material needed by the Navy. "A" school training takes twenty weeks at Fort Belvoir, Virginia, and can be supplemented with advanced training in special skills. A civilian printing job would be very similar.

☐ *Data systems technician.* With this rating you would service, maintain, adjust, and repair digital computers, video processors, tape units, and computer equipment. Persons seeking this rating study basic electricity and electronics for eight weeks at Great Lakes, Illinois, then go to San Francisco for twenty-two weeks of "A" school, where they study basic computer maintenance and theory. They can continue in further training if desired. Much of the Navy's computer equipment is used in private industry, so skills acquired in this rating are adaptable to civilian life.

☐ *Air traffic controller.* Navy air traffic controllers are responsible for the safe, orderly, and speedy movement of aircraft in and out of landing areas. You may work on land or on the deck of an aircraft carrier. The "A" school is located in Memphis, Tenneseee, and lasts for thirteen to fourteen weeks. Many civilian controllers have gotten their training in the Navy.

Advanced Training

For those who are willing to enlist for six years, the doors to advanced training are open. The schooling alone may take two years. In these programs the applicants start out two pay grades ahead of the regular enlistees and receive an E-4 grade—petty officer third class—upon graduation. Here is a brief description of three advanced programs.

☐ *Nuclear Field Program.* Following basic and "A" school, you go to the Nuclear Power School in Orlando for twenty-four weeks. Then you are assigned to a six-month on-the-job training program at a land-based nuclear power plant. Once this is completed you are ready for assignment to a surface ship, or, if accepted, to a submarine.

☐ *Advanced Electronics Field Program.* First you go through basic, then you go through twenty-two to thirty-six weeks of "A" school, where you study the basics of electronics systems, magnetic amplifiers, and remote control systems. Once this material is mastered you enroll in more advanced schools and learn about the Navy's sophisticated electronic gear. After that you will probably ship out and work with data systems, communications equipment, or sonar technology.

☐ *Advanced Technical Field Program.* As with the other advanced programs you go through basic, then "A" school, and then more specialized training. In each session you can choose from varied skills to learn.

The following are open to all qualified Navy personnel:

1. *Hospital corpsman:* one of eighteen different specialties among medical technicians.
2. *Radio technician:* operates and maintains submarine radio telegraph and radio teletype machines.

The following are open to men only:

1. *Hull maintenance technician:* performs plate or high-pressure pipe welding, or heat treatment and nondestructive testing of metals.
2. *Interior communications electrician:* submarine communications electrician, automatic telephone and gyrocompass technician, or closed-circuit TV maintenance technician.
3. *Gas turbine systems technician:* maintains and operates gas turbine engines and associated machinery aboard the newer ships in the fleet.
4. *Boiler technician:* operates shipboard equipment that produces steam for propulsion engines and the generation of electric power.

Bonuses

Like the other branches of the service, the Navy occasionally has trouble filling certain positions. This may be because persons with these ratings tend to leave the Navy to make more money as civilians, or because the working conditions are less than desirable. Few people want to work in an engine room, for example, because it is hot, noisy, and usually below the waterline.

To make these ratings more attractive, the Navy offers cash bonuses that are paid after you complete the necessary training. The ratings that have bonuses attached change from time to time as the needs of the Navy change. Here are some ratings for which the Navy has paid bonuses in the past, as well as the amount of these bonuses. To get an up-to-date list, check with your Navy recruiter.

Nuclear fields	$2,000
Boiler technician	1,500
Cryptology technician	1,000

Job List

Following is a list of Navy ratings. The titles and duties change from time to time, so check with a Navy recruiter for up-to-date information. Though most of the jobs are open, in principle, to persons of either sex, women are barred from practicing any of them on combat vessels.

Aerographer's mate
Air traffic controller
Aircrew survival equipmentman
Aviation antisubmarine warfare
    operator
Aviation antisubmarine warfare
    technician
Aviation boatswain's mate
Aviation electrician's mate
Aviation fire control technician
Aviation machinist's mate

Aviation maintenance
    administrationman
Aviation ordnanceman
Aviation storekeeper
Aviation structural mechanic
Aviation support equipment
    technician
Boatswain's mate
Boiler technician
Builder
Construction electrician

Construction mechanic
Cryptologic technician,
    administration
Cryptologic technician, collection
Cryptologic technician,
    communications
Cryptologic technician, interpretive
Cryptologic technician,
    maintenance
Cryptologic technician, technical
Data processing technician
Data systems technician
Dental technician
Disbursing clerk
Electrician's mate
Electronics technician
Electronics warfare technician
Engineering aid
Engineman
Equipment operator
Fire control technician
Gas turbine systems technician
Gunner's mate
Hospital corpsman
Hull maintenance technician
Illustrator-draftsman
Instrumentman
Intelligence specialist
Interior communications electrician
Journalist

Legalman
Lithographer
Machinery repairman
Machinist's mate
Master-at-arms
Mess management specialist
Mineman
Missile technician
Molder
Musician
Navy counselor
Ocean systems technician
Operations specialist
Opticalman
Patternmaker
Personnelman
Photographer's mate
Postal clerk
Quartermaster
Radioman
Religious program specialist
Ship's serviceman
Signalman
Sonar technician
Steelworker
Storekeeper
Torpedoman's mate
Tradesman
Utilitiesman
Yeoman

6. The Air Force

T HE AIR FORCE IS UNIQUE among the services in that its officers are the ones most involved in combat, with enlisted personnel serving a support function. With the leaders on the front lines, so to speak, the Air Force has gained a reputation for ready adaptation to changing situations.

Though smaller than the Army or the Navy, the Air Force is in charge of land-based missiles and strategic bombers, two-thirds of the nation's nuclear arsenal.

The Air Force has over seven thousand aircraft and a total strength of 583,500 men and women.

History

The youngest of the military branches, the Air Force was established in September of 1947. Before that it was a part of the Army.

Prior to the invention of the airplane, the only aerial equipment in the military was the balloon, which was used to gain a high perch from which to observe enemy positions and to direct artillery fire. So it was that the infant Air Force appeared as the Aeronautical Division of the Army Signal Corps in 1907.

During World War I aircraft took a much greater role in battle, and in 1918 the Army Air Service was established. In 1926 it became the Army Air Corps, and this was its name for fifteen years, until it became the Army Air Forces.

During this time aircraft advanced from the fragile planes of World War I to the fighters and bombers of World War II that fought for air superiority over Germany and Japan. The Army Air Forces dropped the first atomic bombs on Hiroshima and Nagasaki, thus ushering in the atomic age.

Finally, in 1947, the Air Force came into its own. A few years later the Korean Conflict saw the first use of jet aircraft by United States fliers; the top ace of that conflict claimed sixteen enemy planes. The Air Force Academy was opened in 1955, and the Air Force began producing its own leaders.

In Vietnam the Air Force flew some of the longest bombing missions in its history, with B-52s taking off from the Philippines, hitting targets in North Vietnam, and then returning. Air Force pilots stationed in South Vietnam worked with the Army in air strikes on enemy forces.

Since Vietnam the Air Force has concentrated on updating the aging B-52 force and building new weaponry based on high technology.

Length of Hitch

Officers. The obligation of Air Force officers breaks down like this, in years:

	Active Duty	Ready or Standby Reserve
U.S. Air Force Academy	5	1
Air Force ROTC	4	2
Officer Training School	4	2

In addition to the initial obligation, other factors can add to the years you owe the Air Force.

□ *Flight training.* Training to become a pilot takes forty-nine weeks, and upon winning your wings you must stay in the Air Force for six more years. If you become a flight officer, such as a navigator, bombardier, or electronics officer, you owe the Air Force four years.

□ *Graduate school.* If the Air Force sends you to graduate school, you have to stay in uniform three years for every year you go to school, to a maximum of four years in the classroom.

□ *Promotion.* When you accept the rank of captain you commit yourself to two more years; the same goes for major. If you accept promotion to lieutenant colonel or colonel you are obligated to serve three more years.

An important note: These add-ons do not have to be served consecutively.

Enlisted. The Air Force offers two enlistment options, a four-year plan and a six-year plan. Every enlistee is guaranteed the training program that is named in the enlistment papers. Here's how the plans look:

Active Duty	Ready or Standby Reserve
4	0
6	0

If you enlist in the reserve, your active duty lasts only long enough for you to take basic training and job training. You then return to civilian life for the rest of the six years to attend monthly drill and two weeks of summer training.

Basic Training

The Air Force has the shortest basic training period of all the services: you're only in for six weeks.

When you first arrive, you and forty or fifty other people are put into a group called a flight. The person doing all of the yelling is the military training instructor.

The Air Force prides itself on being different from the older, more tradition-bound services. The basic training includes no midnight marches, and you spend only one day on the firing range. You are not even issued a pack.

Some things are different in Air Force basic training, but it is just as intense as basic training in the other branches of the service. You start the day with physical training that gets more difficult as time passes and you get in shape. Weight control is important to the Air Force. If you are judged to be overweight and a combination of diet and exercise does not sufficiently reduce your waistline, you will have to go through physical training a second time with a new bunch of recruits, so you will have more time to work off the pounds.

In the classroom you study subjects that focus on the Air Force and others that focus on you. Examples of the former include military justice, discharges, Air Force customs and courtesies, and leaves and passes. Courses with the individual in mind deal with personal finance, drug and alcohol abuse, and health.

A typical day. A day in basic training might go like this:

5:00–6:15 A.M.	Reveille, physical conditioning, and showers
6:15–7:30	Breakfast
7:30–8:30	Dorm preparation for inspection
8:30–11:30	Academic classes
11:30–12:30 P.M.	Lunch
12:30–4:30	Academic classes, drill practice, personal inspection, and retreat
4:30–5:30	Dinner
5:30–6:30	Mail call, briefings
6:30–9:00	Dorm preparation, study time, personal hygiene
9:00	Lights out

All enlisted personnel take basic training at Lackland Air Force Base near San Antonio, Texas. Men and women undergo identical training. They live in different wings of the same dormitory—which is air-conditioned—and are assigned to different flights in the same squadron.

Jobs

Choosing a job begins with the ASVAB, the test you take before joining the Air Force. Once you have an idea of where your talents lie, you can sit down with a recruiter and work out a plan.

Women have particularly good opportunities in the Air Force. Since few enlisted personnel are in combat, the percentage of job categories barred to women, according to the Department of Defense, is only about 2 percent—by far the lowest in all of the service.

You can choose a particular job, or, if you aren't ready to make up your mind, you can sign up for a specific career area. The areas are:

☐ *Administrative Aptitude Area.* This includes positions such as radio operator, freight traffic specialist, and accounting specialist.

☐ *Electronics Aptitude Area.* In this group you will find missile electronics, radar and computer systems, and instrumentation systems.

☐ *General Aptitude Area.* This area covers fireman, printer, computer operator, and medical specialist.

☐ *Mechanical Aptitude Area.* Here you might find yourself doing aircraft maintenance, welding, carpentry, or even piloting a bulldozer.

You may have a hard time making up your mind, but it's generally better to do so *before* you enlist. That way you can make sure you get the job training you really want. Once you're in you are bargaining from a weaker position.

For those who decide to go for a specific job, the choices are wide-ranging. The Air Force has approximately one hundred forty jobs available for enlistees. Here are two of them, along with descriptions, length of training required, and civilian equivalents.

☐ *Cable and antenna installation/maintenance specialist.* People in this job install, maintain, and repair pole lines and aerial cables. Climbing towers and poles is required. They work with underground cable and field wire and related electrical equipment such as control cables, support structures, radomes, and transmission lines.

Following basic training the schooling takes approximately thirteen weeks at Sheppard Air Force Base near Wichita Falls, Texas. The civilian equivalent is a lineman for a telephone company, a cable television installer, or a lineman for a radio and television company.

☐ *Management analysis specialist.* This job consists in compiling and preparing summaries of statistical data reflecting actual versus planned performance toward Air Force objectives. A person in this job compares accomplishments with objectives, determines trends, and maintains data banks.

The training takes nine weeks at Sheppard Air Force Base in Texas. A comparable civilian job is that of a statistical or accounting clerk.

Bonuses

Like the other services, the Air Force uses cash bonuses to entice recruits to fill certain jobs. Many of the positions require extensive training—some more than a year—and to get the bonus you have to sign up for six years.

The specialties that offer bonuses change from time to time as the needs of the Air Force change. To find out what is being offered now you should check with an Air Force recruiter. To give you an idea of what these jobs might be, here are some specialties that rated bonuses in the past, as well as the amounts of those bonuses.

☐ *Cryptologic linguist specialist, $3,000.* This job consists in listening to foreign radio transmissions and recording signals of interest to the Air Force. The amount of training required varies, but it could take as long as seventy-eight weeks. Most personnel with this job are sent overseas.

☐ *Explosive ordnance disposal specialist, $2,000.* This job consists in taking unexploded or damaged missiles or bombs and making them safe. The weapons may be explosive, chemical, biological, or nuclear. If any of the material inside the weapons escapes you must know how to clean it up. The training takes nineteen weeks.

☐ *Morse system operator, $1,000.* This specialist operates radio receivers and typewriters to send and receive coded messages. The training lasts twenty-one weeks.

Job List

The following are most of the jobs the Air Force offers to enlistees. Those that are barred to women are marked with an asterisk. The titles and the duties change from time to time. Your Air Force recruiter will have up-to-date information.

Mechanical Aptitude Area

Aerospace ground equipment
  mechanic
Air cargo specialist
Aircraft armament systems
  specialist
Aircrew egress systems
  mechanic
Aircraft environmental
  systems mechanic
Aircraft fuel systems
  mechanic
*Aircraft loadmaster
Airframe repair specialist

Aircraft pneudraulic systems
  mechanic
Airlift/bombardment aircraft
  maintenance specialist
Cable and antenna installation
  and maintenance specialist
Cable splicing installation and
  maintenance specialist
Construction equipment
  operator
Corrosion control specialist
Cryogenic fluids production
  specialist

Electrical power production
specialist
Environmental support
specialist
Explosive ordnance disposal
specialist
Fabrication and parachute
specialist
General-purpose vehicle
mechanic
Heating systems specialist
Helicopter mechanic
Jet engine mechanic
Liquid fuel systems
maintenance specialist
Machinist
Marine engine specialist
Masonry specialist
Metal fabricating specialist
Metals processing specialist
Missile maintenance specialist
Munitions systems specialist
Pavements maintenance
specialist
Plumbing specialist
Protective coating specialist
Reciprocating propulsion
mechanic
Refrigeration and
air-conditioning specialist
Seaman
Special vehicle mechanic
Tactical aircraft maintenance
specialist
Turbo-prop propulsion
mechanic
Vehicle body mechanic
Vehicle operator/dispatcher

Administrative Aptitude Area

Administration specialist
Airfield management specialist
Air passenger specialist
Chapel management specialist

Contracting specialist
Disbursement accounting
specialist
Freight traffic specialist
General accounting specialist
Ground radio operator
Inventory management
specialist
Morse systems operator
Operations system
management specialist
Passenger and household
goods specialist
Personal affairs specialist
Personnel specialist
Printer systems operator
Real estate cost management
analysis specialist
Recreation services specialist

General Aptitude Area

Aeromedical specialist
Aerospace control and
warning systems operator
Aerospace physiology
specialist
Aircrew life support
specialist
Air traffic control operator
Audiovisual media specialist
Club management specialist
Command and control
specialist
Computer operator
Continuous photo-processing
specialist
Dental assistant specialist
Dental laboratory specialist
*Defensive aerial gunner
Diet therapy specialist
Duplicating specialist
Education specialist
Electronic intelligence
operations specialist
Entomologist

Environmental health
specialist
Fire protection specialist
Food service specialist
Fuel specialist
Geodetic surveyor
Graphics specialist
Imagery interpreter specialist
*In-flight refueling operator
Information specialist
Instrumentalist
Instrumentalist technician
Intelligence operations
specialist
Law enforcement specialist
Maintenance analysis
specialist
Management analysis
specialist
Materiel facilities specialist
Meatcutter
Medical administrative
specialist
Medical laboratory specialist
Medical materiel specialist
Medical service specialist
Mental health clinic specialist
Mental health ward specialist
Motion picture camera
specialist
Nondestructive inspection
specialist
Occupational therapy
specialist
Packaging specialist
*Pararescue/recovery specialist
Pharmacy specialist
Photolithography specialist
Physical therapy specialist
Printing-binding specialist
Programming specialist
Radio and TV broadcasting
specialist
Radio communications
analysis/security specialist
Radiologic specialist

Safety specialist
*Security specialist
Site developer
Small arms specialist
Still photographic specialist
Survival training specialist
*Tactical air command and
control specialist
Target intelligence specialist
Telecommunications
operations specialist
Veterinary specialist
Voice processing specialist

Electronics Aptitude Area

Aerospace photographic
systems specialist
Airborne
meteorological/atmospheric
research equipment
specialist
Airborne warning and control
radar specialist
Aircraft electrical systems
specialist
Aircraft control and warning
radar specialist
Air traffic control radar
specialist
Analog flight simulator
specialist
Analog navigation/tactics
training devices specialist
Automatic flight control
systems specialist
Automatic tracing radar
specialist
Avionic communications
specialist
Avionic inertial and radar
navigation systems specialist
Avionic navigation systems
specialist
Avionics aerospace ground
equipment specialist

Avionic sensor systems specialist

Biomedical equipment maintenance specialist

Bomb-navigation systems mechanic

Defensive fire control systems mechanic

Defensive systems trainer specialist

Digital flight simulator specialist

Electrician

Electric power line specialist

Electronic communications and cryptographic equipment systems specialist

Electronic computer systems specialist

Electronic-mechanical communications and cryptographic equipment systems specialist

Electronic switching systems specialist

Electronic warfare systems specialist

Ground radio communications equipment specialist

Instrumentation mechanic

Instrument trainer specialist

Integrated avionic communications, navigation, and penetration aids systems specialist

Integrated avionics attack control systems specialist

Integrated avionics component specialist

Integrated avionics computerized test station and component specialist

Integrated avionics elect warfare equipment and component specialist

Integrated avionics instrument flight control systems specialist

Integrated avionics manual test station and component specialist

Integrated avionics systems specialist

Missile control communications specialist

Missile electronic equipment specialist

Missile systems analyst specialist

Missile systems maintenance specialist

Missile trainer specialist

Missile warning and space surveillance sensor repair specialist

Navigational aids equipment specialist

Nuclear weapons specialist

Precision imagery and audiovisual media maintenance specialist

Precision measuring equipment specialist

Radio relay equipment specialist

Space communications systems equipment operator/specialist

Space systems equipment specialist

Telecommunications systems control specialist/attendant

Telecommunications systems equipment maintenance specialist

Telephone equipment installation and repair specialist

Telephone switching equipment specialist electro/mechanical

Television equipment specialist

Weapon control systems mechanic

Weather equipment specialist

7. The Marine Corps

IF ONE WORD COULD BE USED to describe the Marine Corps, that word would be versatile. Marines have the longest basic training of all the services, and they are prepared to fight under a variety of conditions by themselves or in close cooperation with the Army, Navy, or the Air Force.

The Corps prides itself on being able to deploy troops on short notice, and for this reason Marines are known as the "first to fight."

The smallest of the Department of Defense branches, the Marine Corps has 193,400 men and women in uniform.

History

The Marines have always been linked to the Navy. The Continental Congress established the Marine Corps in 1775, and for a time Marines served only on ships. When an

American warship would engage in battle with that of an enemy, the Marines would swarm aboard the other vessel and engage in hand-to-hand combat.

It was not until 1834 that separate companies were formed on land, and thereafter the Marines could fight alongside the Navy and the Army. The Corps has participated in every U.S. war, including the War of 1812, the Mexican War (from which the line about the "halls of Montezuma" in the Marines' Hymn comes), and the Spanish American War.

The Marines fought well in World War I, but it was with the many amphibious landings of World War II that the Corps truly distinguished itself. Having the capability to come in from the sea, establish a beachhead, and keep moving, the Marines led the American advance toward Japan.

Since World War II the role of the Marines has expanded. They fought alongside the Army in Korea and Vietnam, and they have been sent by presidential order to such places as the Dominican Republic and Lebanon, and to an island off Cambodia to rescue a captured American cargo ship.

Currently the Marines guard U.S. embassies, naval installations, and ships, but their primary function is readiness. "Let it be known," said the commandant of the corps, "that, when called, Marine forces will fight our country's battles in the configuration most useful to our nation."

Length of Hitch

Officers. All commissioned officers are obliged to serve the Corps for a specific number of years. After that they can resign and return to civilian life or serve in the Ready Reserve.

The obligations break down like this, in years:

	Active Duty
U.S. Naval Academy	5
Naval Reserve Officer Training Corps	4
Officer Candidate Class	3

The three- to five-year obligation is for your initial officer training. If you want more training from the Corps, the opportunity is there—but your obligation will increase.

Here are some of the opportunities for officers along with the increased obligations.

☐ *Graduate school.* If you want to get an advanced degree and the Marine Corps sends you to graduate school, you have to stay in uniform three years for the first twelve months of schooling and one more year for any time over twelve months, to a maximum of eighteen months. If, for example, you enter a fifteen-month Master's program in Business Administration, you owe the Marines four years.

☐ *Promotion.* If you accept a promotion to the next rank you commit yourself to two more years.

☐ *Aviation training.* In the Marines you can fly jet fighters, helicopters, or multi-engine transports. Pilot training (under Navy supervision) takes about one and a half years, and once you get your wings you owe the Marine Corps four and a half years.

An important note: These add-ons are not always cumulative. This means if you were to go through Naval ROTC and then through pilot training you would not owe the Marine Corps ten and a half years. If you entered flight training as soon as possible, your obligation after winning your wings would be only four and a half years.

Enlisted. Men who join the enlisted ranks of the Marine Corps sign up for six years. Women, unlike men, do not have to serve in the reserve after leaving active duty. How a man's six years are spent, however, depends on the program he selects.

Here are the options, in years, for the active Marines:

Active Duty	Ready or Standby Reserve
3	3
4	2
6	0

And for the Marine Corps Reserve:

	Active Duty	Ready Reserve	Standby Reserve
Women only	⅓–1	3	3
Men and women	⅓–1	4	2
Men and women	⅓–1	6	0

The length of active duty required of those enlisting in the reserves depends on the kind of schooling taken after basic training.

Basic Training

While the other branches of the military soft-pedal their basic training, the Marines thrive on their tough reputation. Basic training, or boot camp, lasts for ten weeks—the longest in the service—and is taken either at Parris Island, South Carolina, or in San Diego, California.

Women's basic training is offered only at Parris Island and lasts for eight weeks. Women have a shorter training period because they are barred from taking part in combat and therefore do not have to learn battlefield skills.

Recruits are assembled in platoons of fifty-five to seventy-five and placed under the supervision of a drill instructor. Then the training begins in earnest. Activities in boot camp begin at 5:00 A.M. and run until 9:00 P.M. Six days a week future Marines face ten hours of training, three hours of meals, two hours of administrative work, and one hour to themselves. On Sunday platoons sometimes relax by competing against each other in events such as the tug of war, 2-mile relay, 100-yard dash, fireman's carry, pushups, and pullups.

The training is broken down into three phases. In the first phase the recruits work on physical conditioning, close-order drill, first aid, guard duty, personal hygiene, and Marine Corps history and traditions. On the physical side, these first three weeks include a progressively harder program of calisthenics and individual and formation runs, as well as the obstacle course and a special exercise known as the confidence course.

The recruits are also introduced to the M-16 rifle, and with it they begin close-combat training. Part of the instruction includes use of the pugil stick, a padded stick used to teach bayonet fighting. Recruits wear football helmets and other protective gear during this exercise, but it remains one of the more physically demanding parts of boot camp.

The second phase concentrates on the use of the M-16 and consists of two weeks on the rifle range. Recruits learn to clean the rifle, to fire it at targets as far away as 500 yards and to take it apart in the dark.

The final training phase sees the Marines-to-be in the field practicing battle skills such as offensive and defensive combat, day and night movement, and techniques of amphibious and helicopter assault.

The physical training that has continued since day one is increased, with recruits running up to three miles a day, climbing ropes, and going through an obstacle course with increasingly difficult challenges.

The physical part: men. The exercises, running, and seemingly endless pushups culminate in the Physical Fitness Test, in which men must complete minimum requirements in three events: the pullup, the bent-knee situp, and the three-mile run. Recruits aren't the only ones who have to take this test. All Marines—officers and enlisted—take it every six months; the Corps believes in keeping fit.

Here are the minimum acceptable performances:

Age	Pullups	Situps	3-Mi. Run (min.)	Passing Score
17–26	3	40	28	135
27–39	3	35	29	110
40–45	3	35	30	85

You get extra points for any pullups or situps above the minimum and for a shorter time on the three-mile run. You have to complete the minimum number in each group and then get enough extra points to meet the passing score. One hundred thirty-five is barely passing; to get a first-class rating you have to score 225.

The physical part: women. The system is the same as the men's, although the events are different. Instead of pullups women perform a flexed-arm hang, and instead of a three-mile run women only have to cover one and a half miles.

Here is the point system:

Age	Flexed-Arm Hang (sec.)	Situps	1½-Mi. Run (min.)	Passing Score
17–25	16	22	15	100
25–31	14	20	16	82
32–38	12	18	17	64

One hundred points is barely passing; to score first class you must have 200 points.

Basic training for men and women ends when they successfully qualify in three of the following: an inspection by the battalion commander, the physical fitness test, a comprehensive final exam on Marine matters, and marksmanship.

After graduation the trainee is no longer a recruit; he or she will now be addressed as a United States Marine.

Jobs

The Marine Corps has thirty occupational fields comprising over one hundred sixty jobs that are open to enlistees right after boot camp. Like the Army, the Marines call each job a Military Occupational Specialty, or MOS.

You and the recruiter sit down with your ASVAB scores and figure out the jobs for which you qualify. The Marines have a large number of combat positions, and one Department of Defense study estimates that 4 percent of Marine MOS's are barred to women.

Once you arrive at a decision, the Marine Corps guarantees you'll get the training. After boot camp you'll report to one of the Marine schools across the country and begin training.

Here are three career fields and some of the jobs that fall in them as well as the length of training for each.

☐ *Audiovisual*. Marines in this job field operate still and motion picture equipment, process film, and print photographs. They may also repair cameras and edit films.

Graphics specialist	12 weeks
Audio/TV production specialist	12 weeks
Still photo specialist	12 weeks

☐ *Utilities*. Men and women in this field install, operate, and maintain electrical, water supply, heating, and plumbing equipment, as well as working with refrigeration and air conditioning machinery.

Basic refrigeration mechanic	7 weeks
Basic electrician	7 weeks
Basic plumbing and water supplyman	7 weeks

☐ *Public Affairs*. These Marines gather information and write news stories, historical pieces, and radio and television scripts.

Information specialist (broadcaster)	10 weeks
Information specialist (journalist)	10 weeks

Advanced Training

The Marines have no advanced training for people right out of boot camp. Instead Marines take schooling in their respective specialties and then work in those specialties for a while. At a later point they can take advanced training to become instructors or supervisors.

Bonuses

The Marines offer a $2,500 Combat Arms Enlistment Bonus to people who sign up for certain jobs. These jobs are barred to women, and you have to enlist for at least four years to get one.

Some of the specialties for which bonuses have been paid in the past include rifleman, field artillery batteryman, and assault amphibian crewman.

The Marines also offer a $3,000 Technical Skills Enlistment Bonus. Again, you have to enlist for four years to be eligible. Jobs for which this bonus has been paid in the past include personnel clerk, radio direction finder, intelligence specialist, and weather observer.

To find out what jobs are paying bonuses now you should check with a Marine recruiter.

8. The National Guard

T HE ARMY NATIONAL GUARD and the Air National Guard are perhaps the least understood of the nation's military forces. They look like the Army and the Air Force, operate somewhat like the Army and Air Force Reserves, and seem to get called out whenever a civil disorder or natural disaster occurs. No wonder people get confused.

The National Guard is unique in that it has a federal and a state function. For the federal government, the Guard is a group of military men and women who can be quickly put into active duty in the event of war. They have their own equipment and are trained to fight alongside the Army or the Air Force.

For the fifty states, the Guard units represent a disciplined and equipped force that can be called out to assist during hurricanes, earthquakes, forest fires, and any other

natural disasters. When civil disorders occur, such as strikes by
public employees, prison breaks, or riots, the Guard can
rapidly come to the aid of state or local authorities.

There are very few people who serve in the Guard full
time. Most report to their units for training one weekend a
month and go off for extended training fifteen days a year,
usually in the summer. Members of the Guard are seldom
transferred and may not even go out of state. Yet Guard units
have fought in every war, and their training exercises can take
them as far as Europe or the Far East.

Currently the Army National Guard has three hundred
ninety thousand members operating out of 4,933 facilities. The
Air National Guard has almost one hundred thousand mem-
bers assigned to ninety-one flying units and support units.
Airfields and armories are located in the fifty states, the
District of Columbia, Guam, Puerto Rico, and the Virgin
Islands.

History

Army National Guard. The Army National Guard can trace its
history back to colonial times. In fact, some units brag that they
were in existence before the country was. In those days
able-bodied men banded together in militia companies to
protect towns and settlements. When a war came along they
fought in it if they were so inclined. A few militias fought
beside the British in the French and Indian War, and then
fought against them in the American Revolution. George
Washington and Thomas Jefferson at one time commanded
militia groups.

During the 1800s the militias were organized by state,
rather than nationally, yet many of them took part in the War of
1812, the Mexican War, the Civil War, and the Spanish-
American War.

In 1903 Congress passed laws that began to organize these
state militias and to bring their training and equipment into
line with that of the regular Army. The name National Guard
was adopted in 1916.

All this organization took place just in time for World War I. The National Guard supplied seventeen divisions to the American effort, and Guard leaders noted with pride that their men fought just as valiantly as those in the regular Army.

When the war was over the Guard was dormant—until World War II appeared on the horizon. This time around the Guard provided the Army with experienced leadership, and once again the members distinguished themselves in battle. When peace came the Guard was quickly demobilized, and for a period of months it ceased to exist entirely.

The National Guard was reorganized, however, and the Air National Guard was split off into a separate organization. When the Korean Conflict broke out, thousands of Guardsmen were called to duty. Several units were activated during a period of international tension in 1961, and over seven thousand members saw action in Vietnam.

In peacetime the Guard has assisted in various states during floods, forest fires, and other natural disasters. It has also been called out to enforce federal court orders related to school desegregation, to perform vital services when public employees have gone on strike, and to prevent looting during riots.

One high point for the Army National Guard was the blizzard of 1978, which paralyzed cities on the East Coast. The Guard used its manpower and equipment to clear streets and see that emergency personnel got to their jobs. A low point occurred in 1970 when Ohio National Guardsmen killed four students who were a part of a large antiwar demonstration at Kent State University.

For the most part, however, the Army National Guard has served the federal government and the states as a modern version of the old militia companies—an inexpensive but highly effective force that is always ready.

Air National Guard. The first unit in the Air National Guard was established a few months after the Wright brothers convinced the Army that the newly invented airplane had a future in combat. The National Guard aviation units were not used in World War I, although many members found their way into combat through the Army's flying units. When the Guard was reorganized following the war, aviation units were again established.

By the time World War II came along the fliers in the Guard had undergone extensive training, and their presence greatly strengthened the Army Air Corps. In 1947 the name Air National Guard was adopted, and when the Korean conflict broke out over three-fourths of the new organization's members saw action with the Air Force.

Over the years the Air National Guard has served as a support group for the Air Force. At a time of alert, Guard units assist in refueling, transporting cargo, or defending the mainland while the Air Force combat units are deployed elsewhere.

As the Air Force gets new aircraft, the Air National Guard inherits the generation of planes that has been replaced. (Some units, however, use the same equipment as the Air Force.) In this manner the costs of the Air National Guard are kept down, yet the crews maintain a readiness for war.

During the war in Vietnam 9,178 officers and enlisted men from the National Guard were called to duty. Some served side by side with the Air Force over Vietnam, while others manned bases in Japan and Korea.

In peacetime Air Guard units have participated in search missions for missing aircraft, forest fire control, and emergency missions as directed by the governors of the various states.

Length of Hitch

Officers. The vast majority of Army Guard officers come from the regular Army. Since the Guard normally has only thirty-nine days of active duty a year, it is possible for the officers to hold down civilian jobs and still serve in the Guard.

There is room at the top, however, for people who aren't Army officers already. Here are the ways to get there and the obligation incurred.

Qualified high school graduates have three ways of becoming officers in the Army Guard. They can attend the fourteen-week Army Branch Immaterial Officer Candidate Course, the nine-week Reserve Component Officer Candidate School, or a state officer candidate school. Most state programs are taught only on weekends and take more than a year to complete. The obligation for all of these programs is three years.

Most of the officers for the Air Guard come from the Air Force. Others who wish to become officers must attend the Air National Guard Academy of Military Science near Knoxville, Tennessee. A college degree is preferred, but for some career fields it is not necessary. The course lasts for six weeks, and the obligation incurred is three years.

Enlisted. All enlisted personnel in the Army Guard and Air National Guard sign up for a six-year hitch. The longest period they spend in uniform is during the basic training and job training they take in either the Army or the Air Force.

The rest of the six years is divided between active Guard duty, which consists of thirty-nine days a year, and Standby Reserve, which involves no duty and pays no money.

It breaks down like this, in years:

	Basic and Job Training	Ready Reserve	Standby Reserve
Women in Army National Guard only	1/3 –2/3	3	3
All Guardsmen	1/3 –2/3	4	2
All Guardsmen	1/3 –2/3	6	0

Basic Training

The Army National Guard sends its recruits to regular Army basic training. The Air National Guard sends its recruits to Air Force basic training.

Jobs

In theory the number of job possibilities in the Army National Guard is the same as in either the Air Force or the Army, but in practice this is not the case. In the National Guard you join a particular unit instead of an entire branch of the service, and your job possibilities are limited by the function of the unit and the number of skilled people it currently has.

For example, if you planned to join the 134th Refueling Wing of the Air National Guard in Knoxville, Tennessee, you would probably be unable to work as a bomb navigation systems mechanic. A unit needing someone in that specialty might be several states away, and it would probably be impractical for you to join it.

Nonetheless, the training possibilities are there. To find out what skills the units near you need, check with your local National Guard recruiter.

Bonuses

Both branches of the National Guard offer bonuses from time to time to encourage recruits to enter a job field in which there is a critical need. These bonuses can be as high as $2,000. Fields for which bonuses have been offered in the past include military police work, hospital work, and electronics.

9. The Coast Guard

DURING PEACETIME the Coast Guard is not a part of the Department of Defense; it is administered instead by the Department of Transportation. In times of war, however, the Coast Guard operates in conjunction with and under the command of the Navy.

Unlike the branches of the service administered by the Department of Defense, the Coast Guard has a host of duties to perform during peacetime. These include conducting search and rescue missions, enforcing customs and fishing laws, combating drug smuggling, maintaining lighthouses and other navigational aids, controlling pollution, breaking ice, and promoting boating safety.

These missions are performed on the high seas as well as on lakes and rivers. A person in the Coast Guard might instruct small-boat owners about safety on one of the Great Lakes or serve on a massive icebreaker in the arctic.

Currently the Coast Guard has thirty-eight thousand men and women in uniform. Their motto is *Semper paratus*— "Always Ready."

History

On August 14, 1790, Congress authorized the construction of ten boats to combat smuggling. The young republic needed all the tax money it could get, and the Revenue Marine, as the fleet was called, was virtually the only oceangoing force the country had for eight years.

With the exception of the short war on the Tripoli pirates, the Revenue Marine participated in every American war. The cutter *Harriet Lane* fired the first naval shot of the Civil War off Fort Sumter, South Carolina, and the Revenue Service fought in the Spanish-American War in Cuba and the Philippines.

In 1915 the Revenue Cutter Service, as it had come to be known, merged with the U.S. Lifesaving Service to form the Coast Guard. World War I soon followed, and the Coast Guard was called upon to escort ships across the Atlantic and to patrol the U.S. coasts. In proportion to its size the Coast Guard suffered the highest loss of life of any branch of the service in World War I.

Between the wars the Coast Guard returned to its peacetime duties of saving lives, enforcing laws, and aiding navigation. During Prohibition in the 1920s it was charged with preventing people from smuggling alcoholic beverages. This was a thankless task, but it served to build up the Coast Guard to three times its World War I size.

This proved enormously helpful during World War II, when the Coast Guard once again operated as a part of the Navy. Antisubmarine warfare was a prime concern, with U-boats prowling the country's eastern coast, and the Coast Guard once more helped escort convoys across the North Atlantic. The small-boat experience of the Coast Guard was put to use in the island hopping of the Pacific campaign.

The Coast Guard participated in the Korean Conflict, and in Vietnam it worked to prevent the North Vietnamese from bringing in men and supplies by sea.

Since then the Coast Guard has assumed the tasks of combating drug smuggling, enforcing the boundaries of increased ocean territory of the United States, and investigating water pollution. All this is in addition to the full-time work of saving lives, maintaining aids to navigation, breaking ice, and promoting boating safety.

Length of Hitch

Officers. All officers in the Coast Guard have to serve a minimum of six years in a combination of active and reserve duty. The obligation breaks down like this:

	Active Duty	Reserves
Coast Guard Academy	5	1
Officer candidate school	3	3

Certain things add to an officer's obligation in the Coast Guard:

☐ *Graduate school.* If the Coast Guard sends you to graduate school you must stay in uniform two years for every year spent in school.

☐ *Promotion.* Promotions occurring during your initial period of obligation do not increase that obligation. For an elevation in rank thereafter you owe the Coast Guard two years.

☐ *Aviation training.* The obligation for flight training is the longest in the Coast Guard. The training takes approximately one and a half years, and at the completion of training you owe the Coast Guard five more years.

An important note: These add-ons are not necessarily consecutive. If, for example, you finished flight training and received a promotion at the same time, you would not owe the Coast Guard seven years—only the five for flight training.

Enlisted. Everyone who enlists in the Coast Guard must spend six years in a combination of active and reserve duty. It breaks down like this:

	Active Duty	Ready Reserve	Standby Reserve
Active Coast Guard	4 years	2 years	0 years
Coast Guard Reserves			
Reserve Split Training Program (boot camp one summer, job training the next)	9 weeks of basic training; seven weeks of job training	5½	0
Petty Officer Selectee Program	24 weeks of boot camp and job training	5½	0
On-the-Job Training Program	8 weeks of boot camp; 4 weeks of on-the-job training	5¾	0
Direct Petty Officer Program (for men and women 26–35 years old with a skill the Coast Guard wants)	2 weeks of orientation	6	0

In any program you can transfer from the Ready Reserve to the Standby Reserve with the approval of your commanding officer. You serve no duty in the Standby Reserve, and you get no pay.

Basic Training

Groups of approximately sixty men and women make up a company which trains under the supervision of the company commander. Basic training, or boot camp, takes place at Cape May, New Jersey, and lasts for nine weeks.

Recruits quickly learn that although the Coast Guard is not a part of the Department of Defense, the basic training is conducted in a thoroughly military manner.

A typical day. Coast Guard basic training incorporates courses common to all the services and adds a special emphasis on

seamanship and activities that relate to the Coast Guard's
peacetime mission.

A day in the third week of boot camp shapes up like this:

5:15 A.M.	Reveille
5:30–6:00	Physical training
6:00–6:30	Breakfast
6:30–7:30	Barracks cleanup and inspection
7:30–8:20	Company commander decides
8:30–9:20	Human relations course
9:30–11:20	Swimming
11:30–12:20 P.M.	Lunch
12:30–2:20	Military conduct class
2:30–4:20	Communications training
4:30–5:20	Company commander decides
5:30–6:30	Dinner
6:30–9:30	Company commander decides
9:30–10:00	Personal time
10:00	Taps

During the nine weeks recruits master the handling of
small boats as well as the seamanship required on larger craft.
Recruits also spend time on the rifle range. Other topics of
training sessions include:

Officer recognition	History of the Coast
Drug education	Guard
Survival	Personal hygiene
Ranks and rates	Military customs and
Nautical terms	courtesies
Communications	Military conducts
Career counseling	Firefighting
Small arms handling	Human relations
Seamanship	First aid

The physical part. Although the Coast Guard is usually not
involved in combat, some of the day-to-day operations can be
very demanding physically, as anyone who has gone out into a
storm on a rescue mission can testify.

By the end of basic training each recruit is expected to perform the following:

Exercise	Men	Women
Pushups or	20	
pullups	4	
Flexed-arm hang		30 sec.
Bent-knee situps	40 in 2 min.	40 in 2 min.
Jump and reach or	15 in.	12 in.
standing long jump	6 ft. 8 in.	5 ft. 6 in.
300-yd. shuttle run	65 sec.	74 sec.
(25 yd. intervals)		
1½ mi. (optional)	12 min.	13 min.

Jobs

Because it has both peacetime and wartime missions, the Coast Guard offers a wide variety of jobs. Although some of them are very similar to Navy jobs, the Coast Guard does not have the Navy's large number of combat positions. It does have jobs that are not found in any of the other services, such as those related to port security, promoting boating safety, fighting pollution, keeping navigational aids operating, and enforcing customs and fishing laws.

The lack of combat jobs is especially beneficial to women. Unlike in the Navy, where women are barred from serving on combat vessels, it is possible for women in the Coast Guard to serve on or even command the largest ships. In times of war, however, women can be prevented from serving or commanding if the Coast Guard ships operate in a combat zone.

Despite the variety of jobs in this branch of the service, the small size of the Coast Guard means that the typical recruit is not offered a broad choice among them. Thus the Coast Guard does not guarantee job training as readily as do the other services.

To find out what jobs are available at any given time, check with your local Coast Guard recruiter. Here is a partial listing of Coast Guard jobs:

Aviation antisubmarine
warfare technician
Aviation electrician's mate
Aviation electronics
technician
Aviation machinist's mate
Aviation structural
mechanic
Aviation survivalman
Boatswain's mate
Communications
technician
Cryptologic technician
Damage controlman
Dental technician
Electrician's mate
Electronics technician

Fire control technician
Gunner's mate
Hospital corpsman
Machinery technician
Marine science technician
Military policeman
Musician
Photojournalist
Port securityman
Quartermaster
Radarman
Radioman
Sonar technician
Storekeeper
Subsistence technician
Telephone technician
Yeoman

Bonuses

The Coast Guard does not offer bonuses to recruits.

10. How to Get In

O NE OF THE REASONS that military people were so fond of
the draft was that it simplified things. For the most part,
young men were notified it was time to go, they reported to an
induction center, and off they went. Those who wished to
become officers either wangled an appointment to a service
academy, joined an ROTC program, or opted for officer
candidate school. It was as simple as that.

Now that no one is drafted, each of the services has come
up with various enlistment plans to attract potential recruits.
For officers the choices are much the same as before, although
ROTC benefits have been increased.

For enlisted people, however, each service has its own set
of options, many of which are the same across the board. In all
of the branches, for example, you will face six years of active
and reserve duty in some combination. Each branch has a

delayed entry plan, too, whereby you can join up now and report for basic training up to a year later.

The delayed entry plans tie in closely with another future common to all of the military branches: guaranteed job training. They promise that if you want—and qualify for—a particular job, you will be trained for it. They encourage you to use the delayed entry plan so that you will finish your training just when your skill becomes needed.

While all of the armed forces have these two programs, they differ significantly in other ways. Physical requirements are not entirely alike. The number of years on active duty can range anywhere from two to six. Some branches offer cash bonuses for persons who sign up for a particular technical or combat skill. Another branch may offer no bonus for the same skill. The Air Force sometimes offers a choice of base or country.

These plans change quite frequently as the needs of each branch change. If, for example, the Marine Corps finds that plenty of people are signing up for the job of rifleman, then it may remove the bonus from that position and apply it to one for which there is a shortage of people. Or it may drop the bonus entirely.

For this reason the plans discussed in this book will be described in general terms only. To get up-to-date details you need to ask recruiters what is being offered now.

BASIC REQUIREMENTS

Anyone wanting to enter military service has to have a birth certificate and a Social Security card. If you were born overseas of American parents you need to show the recruiter papers that prove your citizenship. Aliens can enter the service, but they must provide proof of lawful entry for permanent residence. You have to be at least seventeen years old to join, and if you are under eighteen you must have permission from your parents or guardians.

A high school diploma is not required except for women entering the Navy, Marines, and the Coast Guard. This doesn't necessarily mean that if you are a high school dropout you will automatically be accepted. If a particular branch of the sevice has many people trying to get in, it may choose those with diplomas over those without them.

Physical Requirements

The possibility of being in combat colors most of the policies and practices of the military. Equipment and uniforms are selected for the worst possible conditions that they are likely to experience.

The same can be said for people in the armed forces. The authorities try to make sure that everyone who gets in is healthy enough to perform in an adverse situation. There is no time during an amphibious assault, for example, to deal with the special problems of a diabetic. And a submarine, which can cruise under water for six months, is not likely to return to port because someone's allergies are acting up.

For these reasons an ailment or deficiency that poses little or no problem in civilian life can be enough to keep you out of the armed forces. When you visit a recruiter he or she will look for symptoms of any condition that might prevent your entering the military. If you pass this preliminary scrutiny, you will report for a more thorough physical examination at an armed forces entry station. Sometimes the physical is given on the same day that you take the aptitude test.

The requirements for getting into the service are much the same across the board, although each branch has special requirements for special types of recruits. Standards for officers are different from those for enlisted personnel. Special programs such as aviation training or submarine duty have tougher standards. You won't, for example, see a six-foot-six-inch fighter pilot; he wouldn't fit in the aircraft.

The military has a long list of conditions that will prevent you from joining up. It has another list of conditions for which you can apply for a waiver. By granting a waiver they acknowledge that you have some sort of problem but decide to take you anyway. One waiverable condition is height. In all the services the minimum height is five feet. You might be a particularly attractive person—with high ASVAB scores or a skill the military needs—yet you're only four feet, ten inches tall. So you get a waiver and they take you anyway, with no plans to put you on the barracks basketball team.

These waivers are often dependent on supply and demand. When enlistments are running high and recruiters are having no trouble meeting their quotas, perhaps no waivers will be given. However, when a particular branch is not getting many people, or not many skilled people, it will often take applicants with waiverable conditions. Oftentimes this happens toward the end of the month when recruiters are feeling the pressure to meet the quota. If you have a condition that you think might cause you problems, then your best bet would be to go in at the end of the month.

Conditions that will keep you out of the military. The following are some of the conditions that will prevent your entering the military. You cannot get a waiver for these problems. For a more complete list, and one that reflects the special requirements of a particular branch of the service, you should check with the appropriate recruiter.

The conditions include:

Drug addiction	Chronic alcoholism
Use of a hearing aid	Braces on your teeth
Diabetes	Drug therapy
Severe harelip	Imbecility
Multiple sclerosis	Muscular dystrophy
Obesity	Malignant tumor
Epilepsy	Severe bee sting allergy
Wool allergy	Severe allergies in general

Conditions for which you can apply for a waiver. The following conditions can also keep you out of the military, but for these you can apply for a waiver. They might be illnesses that you suffered five or ten years ago but have had no recent problems with. If you have had any of these conditions you should supply documents from your physician that explain the extent of the condition or the lack of recent problems. This is not a complete list; for complete details you should check with the recruiter for the specific branch you are interested in.

Hepatitis	Deformity or loss of fingers or
Stomach ulcer	toes
Foot trouble	Somnambulism (sleepwalking)
Hearing problem	Ear surgery
Bone or joint surgery	Surgery on female organs
Asthma	Absence or interruption of
Psoriasis	menses
Enuresis (bed-wetting)	Healed fractures with any
Hernia surgery	plates, pins, rods, or any
Back trouble	device in place

Height and weight requirements. The maximum height for men and women is six feet six inches; the minimum is four feet eleven inches and four feet ten inches. Heights of four feet ten inches or four feet eleven inches are waiverable.

Weight Standards for Men

Height (in.)	Minimum (regardless of age)	16–20 Years	21–30 Years	31–35 Years	36–40 Years	41 Years and Over
58	98	147	153	151	147	140
59	99	152	157	156	152	145
60	100	158	163	162	157	150
61	102	163	168	167	162	155
62	103	168	174	173	168	160
63	104	174	180	178	173	165
64	105	179	185	184	179	171
65	106	185	191	190	184	176
66	107	191	197	196	190	182
67	111	197	203	202	196	187
68	115	203	209	208	202	193
69	119	209	215	214	208	198
70	123	215	222	220	214	204
71	127	221	228	227	220	210
72	131	227	234	233	226	216
73	135	233	241	240	233	222
74	139	240	248	246	239	228
75	143	246	254	253	246	234
76	147	253	261	260	252	241
77	151	260	268	266	259	247
78	153	267	275	273	266	254
79	157	273	282	280	273	260

Weight Standards for Women

Height (in.)	Minimum (regardless of age)	17–20 years	21–24 years	25–30 years	31–35 years	36–40 years	41 years and over
58	90	121	123	124	126	135	135
59	92	123	125	129	129	139	138
60	94	125	127	132	132	142	141
61	96	127	129	135	136	145	147
62	98	130	132	139	141	148	147
63	100	134	137	141	145	151	150
64	102	138	141	145	150	156	154
65	104	142	145	149	155	161	159
66	106	147	150	154	160	165	164
67	109	151	155	159	165	171	169
68	112	156	159	163	169	176	174
69	115	160	164	168	175	181	179
70	118	165	169	173	180	186	184
71	122	170	174	178	185	192	190
72	125	175	178	183	190	197	195
73	128	180	183	188	195	202	200
74	132	184	189	193	201	208	206
75	136	189	194	199	206	214	212
76	139	195	199	204	212	219	217
77	143	200	204	209	217	225	223
78	147	205	209	215	223	231	229
79	151	209	213	219	227	234	231

Waiverable Weights For Men and Women

Height (in.)	Men		Women	
	Minimum	Waiverable to	Minimum	Waiverable to
60	100	90	94	85
61	102	92	96	86
62	103	93	98	88
63	104	94	100	90
64	105	95	102	92
65	106	95	104	94
66	107	96	106	95
67	111	100	109	98
68	115	104	112	101
69	119	107	115	104
70	123	111	118	106
71	127	114	122	110
72	131	118	125	113
73	135	122	128	115
74	139	125	132	119
75	143	129	136	122
76	147	132	139	125
77	151	136	143	129
78	153	138	147	132

ENLISTMENT PROGRAMS

The various branches of the service differ widely in their enlistment programs. In the Army, for example, you can spend as little as two years on active duty, while in the Coast Guard you have to spend four.

The laws of supply and demand cause the branches to change their enlistment programs from time to time as situations change. When recruiting levels are down, the amount of money offered for bonuses goes up, special programs guaranteeing certain options come into effect, and ineffective programs are scrapped. Similarly, when recruitments are running high, bonuses may be lowered or cut entirely, special incentives may be quietly phased out, and standards may be raised.

For this reason it is impossible to list all the current programs here. The *Young Person's Guide to Military Service* can give you an idea of what is offered, but to find out about the current programs you should check with the recruiters for each branch.

Chapters 4 through 9 contain charts showing how your stint in the service can be divided between active and reserve duty. This chapter concentrates on enlistment options that do not concern length of service. First the active forces are covered and then the reserves. Each has a delayed entry plan whereby you can join up now and report for duty up to twelve months later.

Enlistment Programs in the Active Forces

The Army. The age range for people entering the Army is seventeen through thirty-four. Special programs include:

□ *Stripes for Skills.* Applicants who have practiced a skill the Army needs as civilians or have been trained in such a skill in high school or trade school may enlist at the E-3 rank. Later they can be promoted to E-4 ahead of schedule.

The Navy. The Navy accepts applications from people seventeen to thirty-five years of age. Special programs include:

☐ If you have a civilian skill that is needed by the Navy, or if you were a member of Naval Junior ROTC or the Naval Sea Cadets, you can go in at a higher rank.

☐ *Buddy Plan.* If you go in with friends you can undergo basic training together, begin duty at the same station, or both.

The Air Force. The Air Force wants men and women from seventeen to twenty-seven years old in its enlistment programs. Special options include:

☐ *Guaranteed Training Enlistment Program.* Under this plan you select skills from a special list and are guaranteed the first assignment of your choice as well as training.

☐ *Enlistment at E-3.* This is available to those who have completed a three-year Junior ROTC program in high school or who have received the Billy Mitchell or a higher award in the Civil Air Patrol.

☐ *Accelerated Promotion to E-2.* If you choose from a list of critically needed skills you will be promoted to E-2 right after basic training.

☐ *Base of Choice.* This option guarantees those who choose a job from a special list that they will be assigned to a base that they choose from another list and that they will remain there for at least twelve months.

☐ *Country of Choice.* This is like the Base-of-Choice option except you choose a country instead of a base.

☐ *Stripes for College Experience.* If you have 45 semester hours or sixty-seven quarter hours of college work under your belt you can enlist at E-3. Those with twenty semester hours or thirty quarter hours can enlist at E-2.

Marine Corps. The Marines are looking for a few good men and women seventeen to twenty-eight years of age. Special programs include:

☐ *Community College Enlistment Program.* Accelerated promotion to E-5 is available to those who have an associate degree or have completed a special college curriculum in a technical area.

☐ *The Buddy Program.* With this option you and friends of the same sex can join the Marines and be guaranteed that you'll be assigned to basic training together.

The Coast Guard. The Coast Guard wants men and women from seventeen to twenty-five years of age. Their special option is a *Guaranteed School Program.* Qualified applicants are guaranteed a specific training program before they enlist.

Enlistment Programs in the Reserves

As explained in detail in Chapter 3, Reserve forces are composed of personnel and units that can be summoned to active duty quickly in the event of war or a national emergency.

People who join reserve units are on active duty just long enough to go through basic training and job training. After that they return to civilian life and leave it only for their training periods, sometimes called drills, that take place one weekend a month and two weeks in the summer.

The Army Reserve. Men and women from seventeen to thirty-four are eligible to join the Army Reserve. Special programs include:

☐ *Split Training Option.* This is for high school or college students who do not want their basic and job training to interfere with their schooling. You go to basic training the first summer and job training the second. The money you make in the reserve—approximately $4,500 in four years—can help with college costs.

☐ *Simultaneous Membership Program.* With this option you are a member of both the Army Reserve and ROTC while in college. You cannot enroll in this program if you have an ROTC scholarship.

☐ *Stripes for Skills.* If you have a skill the Army Reserve needs you can go in at an E-3 rank.

The Naval Reserve. Men and women seventeen to thirty-four years old may enlist in the Naval Reserve. Several programs involve reserve duty, but the one with the shortest stint of active duty is the *Ready Mariner Program.* You serve anywhere from twelve weeks to about ten months on active duty during training, then you come home to join the local reserve unit.

The Air Force. The Air Force Reserve accepts applications from people seventeen to thirty-four years of age. All recruits have to spend at least twelve weeks undergoing basic training, technical schooling, or on-the-job training. High school students can join the Air Force Reserve and participate in as many as twenty-four individual training periods with pay before undergoing basic training.

The Marine Corps. Men and women seventeen to twenty-eight years old may enlist in the Marine Corps Reserve. They go to boot camp with other Marines and then take job training. This process takes anywhere from four and a half to twelve months, depending on your choice of job training. You can split the training, going to boot camp one summer and learning your skill the next. Cash bonuses are available to those who sign up for certain MOS's.

The Coast Guard. The Coast Guard accepts applications from men and women seventeen through twenty-five years of age. There are four basic programs:

☐ *The Petty Officer Selectee Program.* You go first to basic training for nine weeks and then straight into job training. All this takes about four to six months, depending on which job you select. After this period you spend the rest of your time in monthly drills and the annual two-week training.
☐ *The Petty Officer Summer Program.* This is much the same as the one above, except you take basic training one summer and job training the next. Between summers you attend monthly drills.

☐ *On-the-Job Training Program.* This one has the shortest training time of all the Coast Guard offerings for young people who have had no prior military service. You spend nine weeks in boot camp and four weeks in on-the-job training. Then it's back home for the monthly and annual drills.

Army and Air National Guard. At this time the Army and Air National Guard offer no special enlistment programs besides those described in Chapter 8.

11. How to Become an Officer

IF YOU WANT TO MAKE the military your career it makes sense to go in as an officer. You will receive more pay, more responsibilities, and a greater opportunity for advancement. Even if you plan to stay in the military for only a short time it is worthwhile to join the officer corps. Military officers often gain managerial experience and advance in rank more quickly than their civilian counterparts. The officer corps also offers opportunities to inexpensively further your education. This, plus the managerial experience you gain, can be very useful when you leave the military and apply for a civilian job.

Virtually all officers start off at the lowest rank—second lieutenant in the Army, Air Force, and Marine Corps, or ensign in the Navy and Coast Guard. There are three ways of becoming an officer: through a service academy, through ROTC, or through an officer candidate school (OCS). A fourth way is by direct appointment, but this is reserved for persons in professions the military needs, such as doctors, lawyers, or chaplains.

THE SERVICE ACADEMIES

If you are thinking about becoming an officer, then the four service academies are the best place to begin. Whether they come from the Military Academy (West Point), the Naval Academy (Annapolis), the Air Force Academy, or the Coast Guard Academy, graduates of these elite schools are the cream of the officer corps.

American history is illuminated with the names of men who came from service academies. Robert E. Lee, Ulysses S. Grant, Douglas MacArthur, Dwight Eisenhower, George Patton, Chester Nimitz, Hyman Rickover, and Jimmy Carter are some of the generals, admirals, and presidents who once wore cadet uniforms.

If you are accepted to one of the academies you get four years of college for free, plus pay, medical care, and room and board. Unlike your counterparts in ROTC, you receive an entire curriculum that is aimed toward military service. Once you graduate you are given first crack at choice assignments such as aviation and submarine duty.

Even more important, the academies form the ultimate "old boy network" in the military—a network that will swing into action when promotions and assignments are up for grabs. It's no wonder that academy graduates, having had helping hands along the way, are the top leaders in almost every branch of the service.

The academies emphasize the strong character and leadership qualities of their graduates and constantly stress that cadets are very special people. In one sense they *have* to be special people; they put up with a system in effect at only a handful of colleges in this country.

First of all, it is very difficult to get in. A complicated process pits applicants against each other in securing nominations from a variety of high governmental officials. Once a young person receives a nomination, he or she may have to survive another round of competition to get in. Academic records, athletics, and the all-important leadership qualities are scrutinized in deciding who gets in.

The only exception to this is the Coast Guard Academy, which has no appointments, quotas, or special admissions categories. Everyone who wants to get in participates in one competition.

Once in—no matter which academy—it's no picnic. Freshmen are subjected to a degree of harassment that would never be tolerated at a conventional school. The physical and psychological pressure is intense, much as in boot camp, except it lasts for the entire first year. At West Point alone, over 35 percent of the students do not make it to graduation.

Cadets must adhere to an honor code that requires them to leave for the slightest infraction of the rules. Cadets have been removed from academies for suspecting others of breaking the rules and not reporting it to their superiors. In addition, all cadets must participate in athletics—like it or not—on an intercollegiate or intramural level.

The academic training at a military academy concentrates on "the art and science of warfare" and thus is more limited than that of a conventional college. Sometimes the faculty, though they be high-ranking officers, do not have the academic credentials that one might find among professors at an equally selective civilian college.

After graduation the newly commissioned officers are faced with an obligation for five years of active duty—the longest of any beginning officers.

Perhaps the best way of determining whether you would like to go to an academy is to visit one or more of them. Actually walking the grounds and talking with cadets can reveal the good points and the bad in a way that no brochure or book ever can. All of the academies encourage visitors, especially those who are considering applying for a nomination.

In addition, all of the academies have liaison officers around the country who can answer your questions and guide you through the complicated application procedure. You can get the name of the officer nearest you by writing the appropriate academy.

Brochures for the four academies clearly point out that cadet life is not for everyone. Despite this, thousands of high school students apply every year, and the academies are never at a loss for qualified students from which to choose. If you find out too late that a service academy is no place for you, you can resign during the first two years and incur no military obligation.

West Point. The United States Military Academy is located on sixteen thousand acres of land on the West Point of the Hudson River, about fifty miles north of New York City. It was established in 1802, making it the oldest of the service academies. The first class had ten cadets.

Now West Point has approximately forty-five hundred cadets. Each receives a general education in mathematics, science, engineering, English, history, social sciences, national security, and psychology. Cadets have a choice of two tracks of study: a mathematics-science-engineering track and a humanities–public affairs track.

During the summers cadets master such things as artillery firing, mountaineering, wilderness survival, and tank operations. They may take jungle warfare training in Panama or northern warfare training in Alaska; they may learn to pilot a helicopter or use a parachute.

Annapolis. The United States Naval Academy is located on 329 acres of land in Annapolis, Maryland, on the Chesapeake Bay, about ten miles from Washington, D.C. It was established in 1850.

Annapolis has forty-five hundred midshipmen, as cadets are known. It trains officers for both the Navy and the Marine Corps. "Middies" study mathematics, science, social studies, and the humanities. At least 80 percent of the midshipmen must major in engineering, math, or science-oriented disciplines. The rest can major in the humanities or social sciences.

In the summer after their first year of study midshipmen go to sea with fleets in the Atlantic, Pacific, or Mediterranean.

There they become familiar with life at sea and assume some leadership positions. The following summer they may participate in aviation, submarine, or Marine Corps training, and the next year they go back to sea and practice celestial navigation, weapons training, and basic fleet tactics.

Air Force Academy. The newest of the military academies is located on eighteen thousand acres of land near Colorado Springs, Colorado. It opened in 1955 with a class of 306 cadets.

Now there are 4,523 cadets at the Air Force Academy— 4,423 men and 100 women. They take courses in science and engineering as well as in the social sciences and humanities. There are specific majors in each field, yet cadets can elect a nonmajor path through a wide variety of courses.

Summers find cadets taking training in survival, evasion, resistance, and escape in the Rocky Mountains. Later they can serve at Air Force installations to experience and observe life in the active Air Force and participate in activities such as soaring, parachuting, light-plane flying, and navigation training.

Coast Guard Academy. The smallest of the service academies, the Coast Guard Academy is located on one hundred acres at the mouth of the Thames River in New London, Connecticut. It was founded in 1877, and it now accommodates nine hundred cadets.

The cadets have a choice of nine majors: civil, electrical, marine, or ocean engineering; marine, mathematical, or physical science; government; or management.

During the summers cadets take a long cruise on the *Eagle*, a three-masted sailing ship, or on a Coast Guard cutter. They are trained in seamanship, navigation, damage control, and fire fighting. They assist in day-to-day operations at Coast Guard installations and sometimes take cruises to foreign ports.

Eligibility

To qualify for admission to any of the service academies you must be a U.S. citizen who is at least seventeen years old but not yet twenty-two years old on July 1 of the year you plan to enter. You cannot be married or plan to marry during your four years at an academy, and you cannot have any dependents. In considering whom to accept, the admissions staff looks at the whole candidate, taking into account academics, physical fitness, and leadership qualities.

Since all of the academies lean toward science and engineering majors, applicants are urged to take four years of math and plenty of science in high school. Students may take either the American College Testing Program (ACT) test or the Scholastic Aptitude Test (SAT) of the College Board Admission Testing Program. And it always helps to have good grades.

Sports and physical conditioning are a big part of academy life; students must participate in intercollegiate or intramural sports. Anyone seeking a nomination must undergo an extensive physical examination—one with the highest standards in the military. Participation in varsity or other sports in high school is very helpful in getting in. Out of the 1541-member class of 1985 at West Point, for example, 1268 cadets won an athletic letter while in high school.

Obviously, people who plan to become officers should be good leaders. Each academy looks closely at how many offices you held in high school organizations or how many teams you captained. Participation in scouting, church, or civic activities is also considered.

Because of the academies' whole-candidate approach, it is possible that an applicant with low grades but with very high leadership potential can still get in. The same goes for someone who has perfect grades but is weak in athletics. As with all colleges, fielding winning intercollegiate teams is important. If you are an All-American pass receiver or a winning quarterback, you may find it downright easy to get into a service academy.

Obtaining a Nomination

Unless your father was a Medal of Honor winner in one of the services, you will have to secure a nomination from an elected or military official to be considered for admission to any service academy except the Coast Guard's.

Admissions officers at the academies urge that interested students apply for nominations no later than the spring of their junior year in high school. You should apply in all of the categories for which you are eligible. Congressional appointments are the most important; by law the first 150 appointments to any academy and three-fourths of the remainder must be congressional nominees.

You do not have to know your senator or representative personally to obtain a nomination. Most elected officials diligently seek the best qualified candidates from their district. Politics, however, sometimes enters these nominating procedures. If your mother was a campaign treasurer for someone who tried to defeat your congressman, then you might have a hard time securing a nomination from that particular official.

If you have your sights on a service academy, it's not a bad idea to approach your senator or representative before it is time to ask for the nomination. You might do this by writing to him, working in a campaign for him or his party, or visiting him in his local or Washington office. It can't hurt.

Once you've determined you are eligible and decide you want to go, you should apply to one or more of the following:

☐ *U.S. senators and representatives, the delegate from the District of Columbia, and the resident commissioner of Puerto Rico.* These officials can have five men or women attending each of the academies at one time. If all five spots are filled, no nominations can be made until someone graduates and a place opens up. For each vacancy, ten persons can be nominated. You should apply to the appropriate official for a nomination.

☐ *The president of the United States.* The president can make up to 100 appointments a year to each academy, but the applicants must be the children of career members of the armed forces (including the Coast Guard) who are on active duty, retired, or deceased. You should apply to the superintendent of the appropriate academy, and not to the president directly.

☐ *The vice president of the United States.* The vice president can have five people from the country at large attending each of the academies. Whenever there is a vacancy from one of these spots, the vice president can nominate ten applicants. This is the most competitive nomination, and you should apply to the Office of the Vice President, Washington, D.C., 20510 by September 1 of your senior year in high school.

☐ *The governors of Puerto Rico, the Canal Zone, and American Samoa, and the delegates from Guam and the Virgin Islands.* Each of these officials may have one person in attendance at each academy. The governor of Puerto Rico nominates natives of the island, whereas the resident commissioner of Puerto Rico nominates residents of the island. In each case you should apply to the officeholder directly.

If you fall into one of the following categories, you need not secure a nomination from an elected official.

☐ *Regular Army, Navy, Air Force, Marine Corps personnel.* They are eligible if they have completed one year of active duty by July 1 of the year they wish to enter an academy. They should apply to the commanding officer to compete for 85 appointments at each academy.

☐ *Reserve Army, Navy, Marine Corps, and Air Force personnel.* These applicants must be on active duty or belong to a drilling unit, and they must have served in the reserve for at least one year prior to July 1 of the year they wish to enter. They apply to commanding officers to compete for 85 appointments to each academy.

☐ *ROTC members.* These applicants compete for ten appointments at each academy. They should apply through their professor of military science.

☐ *Students at honor naval and military schools.* These military prep schools will be discussed later in the chapter. Each headmaster nominates three applicants, who compete for ten appointments at each academy. Apply to the appropriate headmaster.

☐ *Children of deceased or disabled veterans and children of prisoners of war or persons missing in action.* Children of military personnel who were killed in action or who died or were totally disabled from wounds, injuries, or disease received while on active duty are eligible, as are the children of servicemen or civilians who are prisoners of war or missing in action. Apply to the superintendent of the intended academy. A maximum of sixty-five appointees may be at one academy. Anyone who is eligible for this category is barred from competing for the presidential nominations.

☐ *Children of Medal of Honor winners.* These applicants have the best chance of all, for if they are qualified they are automatically admitted, and there is no limit to the number of positions available to them.

The Vice President, congressmen, governors, the delegate from the District of Columbia, and the commissioner of Puerto Rico can use any method to select their nominees. Some use civil service screening examinations. Most use some variation of the following three methods.

☐ *Competitive method.* This is the most commonly used method and the one the military prefers. The official submits a list of nominees to each academy. The academies examine the records of each nominee and rank them in order of preference. The person ranked highest gets the principal nomination.

☐ *Principal-alternate (noncompetitive) method.* In this process the official makes the selection himself, choosing one person as the principal nominee and ranking the rest as alternates.

☐ *Principal alternate (competitive) method.* Here the official picks his number-one nominee and lets the academies rank the rest.

Just because you are not the principal nominee does not mean you should give up. After all of the reserved spots are filled, the academies will dip into the ranks of the alternates to make up the remainder of the entering class. So even if your congressman has reached his quota for a particular academy, you still have a chance.

And there's always next year. If you can wangle another nomination the academies will consider you once more. For this you need to update your files at the academies to which you have applied. You may decide to go to a prep school.

Military Prep Schools

The Army, Navy, and Air Force operate prep schools for people who would like to go to the academies but feel they need one more year of schooling to meet the admission standards.

Students at these schools fall into two main groups. The first group are men and women who are already in either active or reserve units of the armed forces. They may have been out of high school for a while and need to do something to get back in the academic swing.

The second group is composed of some of the more qualified civilians who received a nomination but were not chosen by the academies. This additional year of schooling gives them an opportunity to improve their academic records, participate in athletics, and demonstrate their leadership abilities.

Getting into one of the prep schools does not mean acceptance into one of the academies will follow automatically. The next year you have to secure another nomination and go through the competition again.

Various branches of the service offer preparatory scholarships to selected prep schools and junior colleges throughout the country. This extra year of schooling can serve the same purpose as a year spent at one of the military prep schools, and it may even be more helpful.

U.S. Military Academy Preparatory School. The Army operates its prep school at Fort Monmouth, New Jersey. Military personnel and civilians who wish to attend must request admission to the school. Write the Commandant, U.S.

Military Academy Preparatory School, Fort Monmouth, New Jersey 07703.

U.S. Naval Academy Preparatory School. The Navy and Marine Corps maintain a prep school in Newport, Rhode Island. Military personnel and civilians do not apply for this school; the Navy looks over the nominees who did not get into the academy and offers selected ones positions at the prep school. Further details about the school can be obtained by writing the Director of Candidate Guidance, Box C, U.S. Naval Academy, Maryland 21402.

The U.S. Naval Academy Foundation offers scholarships to nominees who wish to spend a year at a participating prep school, junior college, or college selected by the applicant. Scholarship applications may be obtained from the Executive Director, Naval Academy Foundation, 48 Maryland Avenue, Annapolis, Maryland 21401. Applications should be received by April 1 of each year.

A similar opportunity for enlisted men and women is offered in the Broadened Opportunity for Officer Selection and Training program, or BOOST. Participants in BOOST receive up to twelve months of academic preparation so they will be better able to compete for an academy appointment or a Naval ROTC scholarship. The school is in San Diego, California.

BOOST is both an opportunity and a gamble. For those already in the service, it is an opportunity to rise from the enlisted to the officer ranks. For civilians it's more of a gamble. To get into BOOST you have to join the Navy first. They can guarantee in your enlistment papers that you'll get the preparatory schooling, but they won't guarantee that you will either get into the academy or receive an ROTC scholarship. And if you don't, you spend the rest of your six-year obligation in the enlisted ranks of the Navy.

The Air Force Academy Preparatory School. The Air Force prep school is located approximately five miles south of the Air Force academy in Colorado. Civilians who were nominated but did not receive an appointment to the academy are automatically considered for admission to the school, but military personnel are considered only if they apply to the school at the same time they request a nomination to the academy. They usually do so, as a way of hedging their bets.

The Air Force has three scholarship funds that help academy nominees to attend other schools. The Falcon Foundation makes annual cash grants for students to attend specific prep schools in various parts of the country. Applications and information can be obtained by writing the Falcon Foundation, P.O. Box 67606, Los Angeles, California 90067. Applications must be received by May 1 of the year you wish to attend.

The Gertrude Skelly Trust Fund offers scholarships only to the children of active, retired, or deceased career members of the armed forces. Applications and information can be obtained by writing the Gertrude Skelly Trust Fund, P.O. Box 1349, Tulsa, Oklahoma 74101. Applications must be in by May 1 of the year you wish to attend.

The Air Force Aid Society sponsors the General Henry H. Arnold Educational Fund, which provides scholarships for the children of Air Force personnel. Applicants can make their own choice of accredited schools. Write for details to the Director, Air Force Aid Society, National Headquarters, Washington, D.C. 20333. Your application must be in by January 31 of your senior year in high school.

The Coast Guard does not have a prep school of its own, but it does reserve fifteen places in the U.S. Naval Academy Preparatory School. These places are offered to outstanding candidates who did not get into the Coast Guard Academy. The Coast Guard also offers ten slots in the Navy's BOOST program.

The Coast Guard Academy Admission Procedures

The Coast Guard has the easiest application procedure; nominations from elected officials are unnecessary. Instead, applicants to the Coast Guard Academy participate in an annual nationwide competition that is based on high school ranking, performance on the ACT or the SAT exam, and leadership potential.

According to the Coast Guard *Bulletin of Information*, each applicant is judged on his or her "academic background, the possession of aptitudes related to both technical and cultural studies, a sincere interest in the Coast Guard as a career, and relevant personality and physical characteristics." The academic portion of the requirements carries a 60 percent weight in the determination, and everything else carries a 40 percent weight.

When all this was put into practice for the 1981/82 academic year, approximately 9 percent of the applicants got in.

RESERVE OFFICERS' TRAINING CORPS

Most of the officers in the armed forces come through ROTC. These men and women attend public or private colleges and take military training alongside their other courses. After graduation they are commissioned into the officer ranks as second lieutenants or ensigns and are obligated for either three or four years, depending on the amount of scholarship money they received from the government while in college.

Some observers think that the ROTC program provides the best officers in the military. Although neither as competitive as a service academy nor offering all its advantages, ROTC gives its members a chance to be a part of both the military and civilian worlds during their college years. By wearing a uniform and participating in military classes and drills, the trainee gets to sample military life before actually joining up. And doing all this in a normal college setting has distinct benefits from the military and civilian points of view.

From the military perspective, ROTC members who are surrounded by civilians have to frequently justify their decision to join the service, and this forces them to think out and articulate their beliefs under sometimes hostile questioning

Late night dormitory exchanges make them clarify the reasons they are planning to enter the military and defend these reasons in a way that cadets at a military academy seldom do.

From a nonmilitary perspective, too, the civilian influence on future officers is an especially important benefit of ROTC. Through contact with professors and fellow students, they hear ideas and arguments that are not always present in a more rigid military setting. They may come away from this marketplace of ideas with a broader view of the world and less of a tendency to view other countries as either allies or enemies.

The result? A well-educated officer whose reasons for joining the military have been tested by fire, whose military training has been tempered by exposure to different ideas, and whose college years have been spent in a more normal setting than that offered by a service academy.

Advantages and Disadvantages

If you are fortunate enough to get a four-year ROTC scholarship, it can be worth as much as $30,000 toward a college education. In these days of rising tuitions and high interest rates, this can be an excellent means of paying for college.

ROTC programs are available at over a thousand institutions of higher learning, from community colleges all the way up to Harvard. Those schools that do not have ROTC programs often have cross-enrollment agreements with schools that do. You can pick an ROTC program at a college that matches your abilities, your geographical preferences, and your educational budget.

If you are not sure about military service, you can try ROTC for two years with no military obligation. If you decide to stay in you may receive a scholarship that pays for tuition, books, and uniforms and includes a tax-free allowance of $100 per month or up to $1,000 per year. Scholarship or not, you stay in the college of your choice and, for the most part, lead a normal student's life. You have the opportunities to meet people and experience things that make up a good college education.

While your school year may not differ much from that of your non-ROTC roommate, your summers certainly will. While your roommate is goofing off or working at a boring job, you can undergo pilot training, ship out on a Navy vessel, or go to camp to practice the things you have learned in textbooks. You will have the opportunity to visit military installations and see what lies ahead.

When at last you enter the military you go in as an officer, with all the privileges and pay that come with the rank. You can travel to exciting places and face challenges that no civilian job can offer, perhaps rising up the ladder faster than your nonmilitary counterpart. After you fulfill the relatively short military obligation, you can return to civilian life or make the military your career. It's up to you.

Then there are the disadvantages. Not all of the ROTC programs will let you major in anything you want; most will restrict you to engineering or science. This is fine if it's what you planned to do anyway or if you have an aptitude in these areas. But you should avoid getting into a subject that you may dislike.

In a related vein, college is a place to learn about yourself as well as the outside world. Many young people enter college thinking they want to do one thing only to find later on that their interests have changed. Within the first two years of ROTC you are free to drop it, but thereafter you are committed to military service. If your plans change, or even if your thoughts about the military change, you are in—and it's very difficult to get out.

If you flunk out of school your plans for becoming an officer go down the drain. But if you are enrolled in the final two years of ROTC you still have a military commitment. A special board reviews your case; it can discharge you or force you to enter the enlisted ranks of the service.

ROTC can be an inconvenience while you are in college. Even while not in uniform you have to keep your hair cut to military standards. On the days you take military classes you have to wear your uniform, and this may bring on good-natured or not-so-good-natured kidding, depending on the atmosphere of your college. You may not be able to participate in activities that conflict with your military ones. Finally, while your room- mates are sleeping late on Saturday mornings, you may be out in the hot sun or cold wind marching and learning close-order drill.

Those summer camps or visits to military installations can throw a rock into plans for work, travel, or the chance to go to summer school. Instead of going to sea during the summer, one Naval ROTC member found himself spending a couple of weeks aboard a ship that never left the dock. He gained some useful experience, but it wasn't quite what he had in mind.

Finally, at the end of your college years your military obligation must be met. It may be three or four years, but it can seem like much longer. Suddenly you are away from civilian life while your friends are going to medical school or law school or starting up the job ladder. If you decide not to make a career of the military, you may feel three or four years behind everyone else when at last you return to civilian life.

Like their counterparts in the enlisted ranks, many ROTC trainees sign up without ever talking to people who are in the service and who can tell them what life in uniform is like. When you first get into ROTC you tend to think only about the benefits; the obligation doesn't confront you until it is too late.

Just like everything else in the military—for enlisted peo- ple or officers—there are some worthwhile benefits, yet they all come at a price.

ROTC Programs[1]

The Army and Air Force each have an ROTC program, and the Navy and Marine Corps have a combined program. Descrip- tions of these follow. The Coast Guard has no ROTC program.

Army ROTC. This program provides college-trained officers for the U.S. Army, the Army Reserve, and the Army National Guard. It is currently offered at more than three hundred host

1. Much of the information in this section comes from *Profile*, a publication of the Department of Defense High School News Service.

institutions across the country with more than a thousand other schools offering Army ROTC through cross-enrollment.

Army ROTC is a four-year program divided into two parts—the Basic Course and the Advanced Course. The Basic Course is normally taken in the freshman and sophomore years. Students who have participated for three years in Junior ROTC, a program conducted at twelve hundred high schools across the country, can get credit for the first year of the Basic Course. No military commitment is incurred during the first two years, and students may withdraw at any time before the end of the second year. Subjects include management principles; national defense; military history; leadership development; and military courtesy, discipline, and customs. Uniforms, required textbooks, and materials are furnished without cost to the student.

After completing this course, selected students may enroll in the Advanced Course during the final two years of college. Instruction in this program includes further leadership development, organization and management, tactics, and administration. Cadets in the Advanced Course receive uniforms, military science textbooks, salary during an advanced camp, and a living allowance of $100 per month or up to $1,000 each year.

The six-week advanced camp is held during the summer between the junior and senior years. This camp permits cadets to put into practice the principles and theories they have learned in the classroom. Successful completion of the advanced camp is required prior to commissioning.

For community and junior college graduates and students at four-year colleges who have not taken Army ROTC during their first two years, there is a special two-year program. Students can enter this program by successfully completing a paid six-week basic camp after their sophomore year and enrolling in the Advanced Course in their junior year. Except for the basic camp, all other requirements for and obligations incurred in the two- and four-year programs are the same.

Under the Simultaneous Membership Program, a person can enlist in the Army National Guard or Army Reserve after high school, attend basic training during the summer, and enroll in the ROTC Advanced Course as early as the freshman year of college. Upon successful completion of the Advanced Course, the cadet can receive an early commission and serve as a second lieutenant with the Army National Guard or Reserve while completing the baccalaureate degree.

Army ROTC offers scholarships for four, three, and two years. Four-year scholarships are awarded on a worldwide competitive basis to U.S. citizens who will be entering college as freshmen. Three-year and two-year scholarships are awarded competitively to students who are already enrolled in college. Students who attend the basic camp of the two-year program may also compete for two-year scholarships while at camp. Two-year scholarships are available on a competitive basis for enlisted personnel on active duty in the Army. These scholarships pay for tuition, textbooks, lab fees, and other educational expenses, and they provide a living allowance of up to $1,000 each year the scholarship is in effect. The value of the scholarship depends on the tuition and other educational costs of the school attended.

Under the ROTC–Reserve Forces Duty Scholarship program, a limited number of two-year scholarships are also available to students who desire to serve in the Army National Guard or the Army Reserve in lieu of extended active duty.

Nursing students may qualify for appointment in the Army Nursing Corps through ROTC. Two-year ROTC scholarships are also available to nursing students. Recipients of these scholarhips serve on active duty after appointment in the Army Nurse Corps.

Scholarship candidates are obligated to serve four years on active duty and two more in the reserve. Nonscholarship graduates may serve three years on active duty and the remaining three in the reserve, or they may volunteer or be chosen to serve on Reserve Forces Duty (RFD). On RFD the active-duty obligation is from three to six months for attendance at the officer basic course, with the remaining time spent in a reserve unit.

Details about the Army ROTC program may be obtained at the ROTC detachment at participating universities or by writing to Army ROTC, Fort Monroe, Virginia 23651. Scholarship forms are available after April 1 each year from Army ROTC, P.O. Box 9000, Clifton, New Jersey 07015.

Naval ROTC. At fifty-seven colleges and universities across the country, Navy or Marine Corps commissions are granted to college students who complete two, three, or four years of naval science study on campus. Two types of programs are offered, for scholarship and nonscholarship students. In addition to students enrolled in the nonscholarship, or college, programs, qualified enlisted personnel on active duty are eligible to apply for the Naval ROTC scholarship programs.

Students compete nationally for the three- and four-year scholarships. Those selected are appointed midshipmen in the Naval Reserve. They may be granted the compensation and benefits authorized by law for a period of not more than four years (forty months). While a scholarship is in effect the Navy pays for tuition, fees, and textbooks and provides uniforms and a subsistence allowance of $100 per month.

Students with advanced college standing who have not taken ROTC previously may compete for two-year scholarships. They are appointed midshipmen in the Naval Reserve upon reporting for enrollment in the Advanced Course. Before starting the Advanced Course they must complete a six-week summer course, equivalent to the Basic Course, at the Naval Science Institute. Those enrolled in the two-year scholarship program have the same privileges and obligations as those in the four-year scholarship program.

Students in the four-year college program are selected from among those applying for enrollment at each Naval ROTC unit. During the first two years, which are spent in the Basic Course, students have the status of civilians who have entered into a contract with the Navy; they can withdraw at any time. Upon enrollment in the Advanced Course, however, students enlist in the Naval or Marine Corps Reserve. The Navy provides uniforms, naval science textbooks, and a subsistence allowance of $100 a month for a maximum of twenty months during the Advanced Course. Upon graduation and completion of naval science requirements, students are commissioned as ensigns in the Naval Reserve or second lieutenants in the Marine Corps Reserve.

Three-, two-, and one-year scholarships are available to students already enrolled in a college program.

Students with advanced college standing who have not taken ROTC during their first two years may qualify for the two-year college program. After successfully completing a six-week course at the Naval Science Institute, they enroll directly in the Advanced Course. Those enrolled in the two-year college program have the same privileges and obligations as those in the four-year college program.

Information about the college programs is available from any of the forty-four Naval ROTC units. Students desiring information about the scholarship programs should contact the nearest Navy or Marine Corps recruiting station or write to the Commander, Navy Recruiting Command, 4015 Wilson Boulevard, Arlington, Virginia 22203.

Air Force ROTC. This program is open to any full-time student at one of the 152 colleges and universities hosting an Air Force ROTC unit, or at one of the 539 institutions that have a cross-enrollment agreement with an Air Force ROTC host institution. Successful completion of either the four-year or the two-year program and an undergraduate degree qualifies a student for an Air Force commission.

For completion of two or more years of Junior ROTC, participation in Civil Air Patrol, military school training, or prior U.S. military service, students may be granted credit for a portion of the General Military Course, which lasts the first two years of the four-year program. Unless they have accepted Air Force ROTC scholarships, students enrolling in Air Force ROTC courses during their freshman or sophomore years incur no military obligation.

After completing the General Military Course students compete for entry into the Professional Officer Course, which is normally taken during the junior and senior years. Admission to the Professional Officer Course is highly competitive.

Students in the two-year program take only the Professional Officer Course. To enter the two-year program a student must have two academic years remaining at either the undergraduate or graduate levels, or a combination of both.

When cadets in the four-year program and applicants for the two-year program enroll in the Professional Officer Course, they also enlist in the Air Force Reserve, which enables them to receive a nontaxable allowance of $100 each month during the school year. In addition they agree to accept an Air Force commission, if offered, after successful completion of the Air Force ROTC program, and to serve on active duty for a period of four years.

Unless they already possess a private pilot's certificate, students qualified to be trained as pilots participate in the Flight Instruction Program. Conducted by a local civilian flying service, this program gives the Air Force an indication of the student's motivation and aptitude for flying. The Air Force pays for all instruction.

Before entering the Professional Officer Course cadets in the four-year program normally complete a four-week field training course at an Air Force base during the summer. Students applying for the two-year program receive six weeks of field training; the additional two weeks are devoted to the academic subjects covered in the General Military Course. The Air Force pays for uniforms, lodging, meals, and travel to and from the training base. In addition cadets are paid about $350 for the four-week camp and about $525 for the six-week camp.

A voluntary on-base summer training program is offered for cadets between their junior and senior years. This program provides specialized career training and an opportunity to experience the kind of leadership and management challenges encountered by Air Force junior officers. Up to twelve hundred cadets may be selected to participate each summer, for either a two- or three-week period. Cadets are paid about $184 for the two-week session and $295 for the three-week session. The Air Force provides meals, lodging, and transportation to and from the training base.

A limited number of volunteers also take part in the Army's Airborne Training Program. This three-week program is conducted at Fort Benning, Georgia.

Sixty-five hundred Air Force ROTC scholarships are available to qualified students in both the four-and two-year programs. Each scholarship provides full tuition, laboratory and incidental fees, and reimbursement for required textbooks. In addition, scholarship recipients receive a subsistence allowance of $100 each month during the school year.

Scholarships for periods of 4, 3½, 3, 2½ and 2 years are available primarily to students in scientific or technical fields. Three- and two-year scholarships are available to students preparing for certain health careers. Limited numbers of two-year scholarships are available to students enrolled in nontechnical fields and nursing.

Candidates for four-year scholarships must apply by December 15 prior to the fall term in which they will enter college. About fifteen hundred high school seniors are offered four-year scholarships each year. Applicants for three-and two-year scholarships should contact the professor of aerospace studies at any institution that hosts an Air Force ROTC unit.

Enrollment in Air Force ROTC is limited to cadets capable of completing all requirements for a commission before reaching a certain age: 25 for scholarship recipients who have never served in the military; 29 for those who have; 26½ for flight trainees; and 30 for missile, scientific, or nontechnical specialists. Waivers may be granted for students in the last group by the Air Force ROTC commandant.

Further details and application booklets about the Air Force ROTC program may be obtained by writing Air Force ROTC/PA, Maxwell Air Force Base, Alabama 36112.

OFFICER CANDIDATE SCHOOLS

The third way of becoming an officer in the armed forces is through OCS. Applicants are enlisted personnel or civilians who have graduated from a four-year college. The civilians join as enlisted personnel, and at the end of their training successful candidates are commissioned as second lieutenants or ensigns.

Gaining admission to OCS is a competitive process, and college students are advised to apply early in their senior year, for it takes several months to decide who gets in. Military personnel should make inquiries through their commanding officer.

OCS training is very intense, much like basic training. It lasts anywhere from three to five months, depending on the branch of the service. If a person continues on with flight training or any other schooling the process may last as long as a year and a half.

Graduates of OCS generally incur an obligation of three or four years; those who continue with flight training usually have to stay in at least five years. Specific information on each branch is available from local recruiters.

Army Branch Immaterial Officer Candidate Course (BIOCC). Civilians who are between nineteen and twenty-nine years old and enlisted personnel on active duty or in the Army Reserve who are between nineteen and a half and twenty-nine years old can apply for this course, which supplies officers for the Army, Army Reserve, and the National Guard. To attend, civilians must have a degree from a four-year college; applicants already in the military must have passed the Army's two-year college equivalency evaluation.

The course lasts fourteen weeks and is held at Fort Benning, Georgia. When their traning is completed the students are commissioned as second lieutenants. They then return to their respective branches, where they are obligated to serve for three years.

Men and women in the National Guard have three options for OCS training. They can take the nine-week Reserve

Component OCS, the fourteen-week BIOCC, or a state OCS program. The state programs last one year, with training taking place on the weekends to minimize interference with civilian pursuits. Requirements vary from state to state; for information check with your local National Guard armory.

Navy Officer Candidate School. Navy OCS applicants have to be between nineteen and twenty-seven and a half years of age at the time of commissioning. The training takes sixteen weeks at Newport, Rhode Island; graduates are commissioned as ensigns and serve in the active Navy or the Naval Reserve. The obligation for active duty is four years, except for persons going into the Supply Corps, for whom the obligation may be either three or four years.

Air Force Officer Training School (OTS). Applicants must be between twenty and a half and twenty-nine and a half at the time of application, and they must be commissioned by the age of thirty. Trainees complete a twelve-week course, and on graduation they are commissioned as second lieutenants in the Air Force. They incur an obligation of four years from the time of graduation. The training is conducted at Lackland Air Force Base near San Antonio, Texas, and graduates serve in either the active Air Force, the Air Force Reserve, or the Air National Guard.

Marine Corps Officer Candidate Class (OCC). Applicants must be between nineteen and twenty-seven and a half years of age, and they must be commissioned by age twenty-eight. The training takes ten weeks at Quantico, Virginia, and graduates are commissioned as second lieutenants. Then they spend twenty-three weeks at the Basic School, a school for officers in Quantico, Virginia, and finally leave to serve an obligation of three years in either the Marine Corps or the Marine Reserve.

The Corps also has a *Marine Platoon Leader's Class (PLC)*, which is available to full-time qualified male freshmen, sophomores, and juniors who are attending accredited colleges. Training is conducted at Quantico, Virginia, and consists of two six-week sessions or one ten-week session during summer vacation.

Upon graduation PLC participants are commissioned as second lieutenants—if they accept their commissions. Unlike participants in the other OCS programs, PLC members can decline to go any further at this point. If they accept the commission, they are sent to the Basic School for twenty-one weeks and then begin their military obligation of three years.

Coast Guard Officer Candidate School. College graduates who are between twenty-one and twenty-six years old can participate in a seventeen-week training program in Yorktown, Virginia. They are commissioned as ensigns and must serve at least three years.

Air National Guard Academy of Military Science. The Air National Guard has its own academy outside Knoxville, Tennessee. One course lasts for six weeks and leads to a commission as a second lieutenant. A college degree is preferred but is not necessary in all fields.

Aviation Training

All of the OCS programs offer some form of aviation training. Generally it takes close to a year to complete, and graduates have a longer commitment than ground officers. For specific details on each program refer to your local recruiter.

Direct Appointments

Doctors, attorneys, nurses, civil engineers, ministers, and persons in other professions needed in the military can receive direct commissions as officers. In some cases the armed forces will enlist a medical or a law student and pay his or her way through school. Direct appointments are made through highly specialized programs, and more information on them can be obtained from local recruiters.

12. Bargaining with a Recruiter

L ET'S SAY YOUR UNCLE owns a used-car lot and offers to give you a car under some unusual conditions. He gives you a choice of any of the cars he has, but once you select one you have to drive it and keep it up for three or four years. No matter how good or bad the car turns out to be, it's all the transportation you'll have for a long time.

If someone gave you a car under circumstances like that you'd probably spend a long time making sure you got the best one. The same thing applies when Uncle Sam offers you a position in the military.

Joining the armed services is much more serious than buying a used car, but the two are alike in several ways. Some people get a terrific deal, whereas others go to the same place and soon find out they have made a big mistake.

The big difference between the military and used cars is that with cars, under normal circumstances, you can get things straightened out; you can always get rid of a lemon and buy a new car. In the military, however, it is harder to straighten things out; you can never simply quit and take up another profession.

In this chapter we'll look at the recruiting process—how it works and how you can get the best deal from it.

The Role of Recruiters

No one has been drafted into military service since 1973. Things were a lot easier for the armed forces before then; they didn't have to make such a fuss about job skills and education benefits. Not much emphasis was put on recruiting at all.

Now things are different. Each of the armed forces has to recruit to keep its manpower at planned levels. Together they spend about $120 million a year on ads, brochures, and other things designed to lure you into the recruiter's office. They are putting some of their best people into recruiting. If you've ever walked into a recruiter's office, you'll see how it works.

Recruiters are friendly people. They drop what they are doing and offer you a chair. They smile and listen to what you have to say. This courtesy and respect can come as a welcome change from the treatment you have received from parents, teachers, or your boss. If you are having problems recruiters listen sympathetically. They offer you some coffee or a soft drink while you talk. They seem genuinely concerned.

At the same time you are looking at them. Whether male or female, recruiters generally look good. They wear clean uniforms with attractive ribbons and sparkling medals. Their shoes glisten. They seem happy in their work—or at least contented.

And when they start to talk, you listen.

You should also begin to think.

Where a Recruiter is Coming From

For the most part, recruiters *are* friendly and sympathetic people. No branch of the service wants to be represented by a grouch. Yet all this friendliness has one purpose—to get you to join the military.

When you ask recruiters about their experiences in the services they will often tell you how good it is—and they are probably telling the truth. People who have a bad time generally don't get to be recruiters. Most recruiters are people who have decided to make the military their career, so it is safe to assume that things have gone well for them.

You should always keep in mind that a recruiter is selling a product—military service. And, like all good sellers, he or she will accent the positive and play down the negative. "If I can bring a guy in with two words, I do," said one recruiter. "If it takes talking to him all day, I do that. But I'm not going to tell an enlistee any of the hard facts of life in case he might walk out the door." Another added, "Let them find out what the facts are after they're in the Army."[1]

All recruiters have quotas. If they bring in the required number of people per month, fine. If they bring in more than that, it looks good on their record. If they can't make the quota, however, things do not go well for them.

Recruiters who do not fulfill their quota get a lot of pressure from their bosses. After all, if the recruiter doesn't produce, the boss looks bad. This pressure takes many forms. Recruiters may be forced to work longer hours or on the weekends. Others have leaves canceled, and some are even threatened with unpleasant duty or an unpopular base.

The pressure from above is worse toward the end of the month, especially if the quota has not been met. Commanding officers may call every hour and chew out the recruiters for not producing enough bodies. Desperate recruiters often have to scrape the bottom of the barrel, signing up people who otherwise wouldn't get in. One Navy officer confided that when sailors repeatedly get in trouble, their records show they were recruited at the end of the month.

---

1. *Military Realities and Guidance Responsibilities*, (Fellowship of Reconciliation). Reprinted from *Militarism Memo*, Fall 1978.

You can imagine how this pressure affects recruiters. If pushed far enough, they may tell you anything to get you in the service and to get the boss off their backs.

Some recruiters will paint a glowing picture of life in uniform. They gloss over minor details such as basic training, long-term overseas duty, and the commitment to the reserves you face when active duty is finished.

In the rush to get you to sign up, a recruiter may lie about job possibilities. The job best suited for you may not open up for eight months, so the recruiter does not mention it. He or she tells you that you should sign up for something else and "change once you get inside."

Young people are often signed up for training they aren't qualified for. Certain jobs require high scores on the ASVAB, and you may not be told your scores are too low for the job you have been promised. Many positions require security checks, and if you have had any brush with the law—no matter how slight—it can be grounds for disqualifying you.

A minority of recruiters resort to illegal means of getting you to join. In New York citizenship papers for 106 Panamanians were forged by recruiters. In Cleveland recruiters had a substitute take physical exams for nine enlistees and mental exams for eleven others. And in Pittsburgh a Marine sergeant signed up a young man who was blind in one eye, another who had polio and a noticeable limp, and a third who was mentally retarded.[2]

If you have a police record or have not completed high school, don't listen to a recruiter who says he or she can fix it for you. Entering the military under false pretenses is against the law and can be grounds for a bad discharge.

Recruiters do get caught and punished for such shenanigans. Last year the Marine Corps alone disciplined fifty-three recruiters for malpractice—and the Marines are the smallest branch of the service.

The one who suffers the most is the enlistee. Once you

---

2. Henry Schipper, "Recruitment Fraud," *Counter Pentagon* (Philadelphia: Central Committee for Conscientious Objectors).

sign those papers it is very difficult to get out. You may find yourself in a combat job that has little value in civilian life, or you may even be discharged with "bad papers." Even if you try to fight what you feel was recruiting malpractice, it will be your word against the recruiter's. And who do you think the military will believe?

Be a Good Consumer

All recruiters are pressured to get you to join, yet only a minority engage in the unfair and illegal practices just described. Even if you find yourself confronting an unethical recruiter, he or she cannot force you to do anything. Military service is voluntary— at least for now—and until you sign up you are in control of the situation. Talking to a recruiter and negotiating an enlistment deal is still like buying a used car—you have to be a good consumer.

Here is a list of things you should keep in mind when you decide to visit the recruiters.

Don't rush into anything. You may have been jilted by your fiancée and may be sick of your job, but don't rush off and do anything in haste. Six years in the military can be a very long time to regret your impulsiveness.

Above all, don't sign anything on your first trip to the recruiters. Don't even think of it.

Make several trips. You are planning to enter a six-year program; surely you have enough time to do it right. The various enlistment options are hard to understand at first. An Army recruiter might say, "You take the ASVAB to determine your MOS before going to basic and AIT." He means you have to take an aptitude test to determine what job you qualify for. Then you go to basic training and job training. Spend a lot of time with the various recruiters so you understand exactly what they are talking about.

Recruiters won't say anything bad about their own outfits, so ask them about the others. A Navy recruiter can be very frank about the shortcomings of the Army and the Air Force. The Marines will gladly point out why you shouldn't join the Army or the Navy, and the National Guard representative will fill you in on all of them.

Note: If you have a police record or any physical problems, or if you haven't finished high school, now is the time to tell the recruiter. He or she is going to find out anyway, and it is better to have everything out in the open.

Talk to people. Don't get all your information from a recruiter. Talk to someone who has been in the service; better yet, talk to someone who is still in uniform. If you don't know such a person ask your friends and relatives for names of people to contact. Christmas and other holidays are good times to catch military personnel at home.

If you are black or latino, make a special effort to talk to black or latino veterans or those still in the service. A white recruiter has little grasp of the problems that face minorities in uniform.

The same goes for women. Recruiters and their brochures don't always emphasize the limitations that women encounter in the service.

Take along a parent or a friend. Once you have gathered the basic information, it's a good idea to take someone along when you begin to ask questions. The recruiter is older than you and can be pretty intimidating sitting there in the uniform. Having an older person along may help in asking the tough questions, and your companion may think of things that you forget to ask.

Take a list of the questions you want to ask. While you are talking your companion can take notes. If you run into an unethical recruiter, he or she will think twice about lying to you when someone is writing things down.

Again, don't get pressured into signing anything right away. Even if you are sure that this is what you want, go home and think about it one more time.

Get the facts about enlistment options. Every branch of the service has a confusing array of enlistment options. You can sign up for anywhere from two to six years of active duty and perhaps get a bonus or some special job training or a definite base in a particular country. It can get quite confusing.

Many of these options have a catch. You may have to enlist for a longer period of time, the bonus may be only for a combat skill that has little use outside the military, or the training may be particularly difficult.

Once the recruiter stops talking, ask these questions:

☐ How long do I have to stay in with this option?

☐ What further tests or physical standards do I have to meet in order to qualify for this option? What happens if I don't meet the standards?

☐ What happens to my option if I can't complete the special training that is a part of the requirement?

☐ If this option guarantees a certain geographical assignment, will I be there the whole time I am in the service?

☐ If I sign up with a friend for the buddy plan, how long do we stay together?

☐ Does this option require a security clearance? What happens if I can't get one?

☐ If it turns out that this option is not available, what other choices do I have?

☐ If I sign up for the delayed entry plan while in school, can I change my mind before active duty begins?[3]

Get it in writing. If the recruiter promises you specific training or any of the various options, have him write it into the enlistment agreement. Spoken promises are worthless. If he refuses to do this, then you should be highly suspicious of what you have heard.

Once more—don't sign just yet.

Get a copy of the agreement and take it home. Talk it over with your parents, a friend, or a veteran. If you don't understand anything on the contract, ask a civilian military counselor—someone who advises people on military matters—or an attorney. Remember—your signature on this document will drastically affect your life for the next several years. Make sure you know what you are getting into.

---

3. *Nine Things to Remember* (Cambridge, Mass.: American Friends Service Committee).

Sign. Once you have negotiated the agreement, understand everything in it, and are satisfied with the arrangements, go ahead and sign. Be sure to get a copy of the agreement and keep it in a safe place.

Everyone feels uncertain after making such a big decision, but you can rest assured you got the best possible deal.

Dealing with a recruiter can be a lot like negotiating with a used-car dealer. The buyer must look out for his own interests. If you rush through the process and sign up without fully understanding what you are doing, the consequences may make you very unhappy. And you will have no one to blame but yourself.

13. How to Get Out

O NCE YOU HAVE TAKEN THE OATH of allegiance, getting out of the military before your period of enlistment is finished is like trying to jump off a moving train. It can be done, but the lasting effects may be much worse than staying on the train until it reaches a station.

Under the law a person cannot simply get out on request. The military has a defined set of conditions that all branches recognize as valid reasons for leaving, but the procedures can vary from service to service and from command to command. Some reasons are pretty clear-cut, such as a medical problem. If you are seriously wounded or cannot physically function, then a discharge is in order.

Note: Information in this chapter was taken from several publications of the Central Committee for Conscientious Objectors as well as official military publications.

Other conditions can lead to a discharge. Some are administrative, as in the case of a recruit who is discovered to be sixteen years old. Other administrative conditions include disability, hardship, security, unsuitability, and a vague one called "for the convenience of the government." Depending on the record of the person involved, he or she may emerge with an honorable discharge in these cases.

Punitive discharges are another matter. These come about following conviction in a military court for a serious offense. It may be a military crime such as being absent without leave (AWOL), desertion, or a particularly bad case of disobedience. Or it may be a crime that would be a felony under civilian law, such as murder, rape, or robbery.

For someone getting out of the military, whatever the reason, the type of discharge is of paramount importance. Like a driving record, a good military discharge may not help you all that much, but a bad one can certainly make life difficult.

Discharges range from honorable down to dishonorable. An honorable discharge entitles you to all of the veterans' benefits described in Chapter 16; other discharges entitle you to fewer or none of these benefits. Since a lot of the financial advantage of serving in the military comes *after* you get out, the system of graded discharge offers considerable incentive to do a good job and hang in there until your hitch is over, no matter how bad things may seem in the mean-time.

Any discharge made under less than honorable condi-tions, or "bad paper," as it is called, will follow you like a dark cloud for the rest of your life. Most job applications ask about military service, and, although a bad discharge won't matter to some people, others will reject you out of hand for having one, no matter how qualified you are for the job.

It is possible to have a discharge upgraded after you leave the service, but you should never count on this taking place.

There are five grades of discharge from the military. Let's start at the top.

Honorable Discharge

If your service has been generally good to excellent in the armed forces and there are no horrendous incidents on your record, you should receive an honorable discharge.

In considering whether a person deserves this highest discharge, the military authorities examine the pattern of behavior and do not focus on the isolated incident. Homosexuals, for example, will get an honorable discharge unless they have been involved in illegal acts. The Army's manual on discharges states that when there is doubt as to whether a person should receive an honorable or a general discharge, the doubt should be resolved in favor of the honorable separation.

General Discharge

A general discharge is also made under honorable conditions, but it is given because a person's record has not been all that good. The person involved may have been a troublemaker, but not such a pain in the neck to deserve a less than honorable send-off. Perhaps the person was not in long enough to establish a record. The young man who is discharged after two weeks in basic training has hardly had time to build up an excellent record. Whatever the case, a general discharge recipient is entitled to full veterans' benefits.

Other-than-Honorable Discharge

Even though this is still an administrative discharge, "other than honorable" speaks for itself. This sort of discharge is frequently handed down for misconduct, illegal homosexual acts, security reasons, or a catchall called "for the good of the service."

An other-than-honorable discharge may cost its holder some veterans' benefits. The Veterans Administration (V.A.) reviews each case on an individual basis, and there is a strong likelihood that the recipient will not receive anything.

The situation in the civilian sector is hard to predict. Although this isn't a punitive discharge, the person who holds it should be prepared to do a lot of explaining.

Bad-Conduct Discharge

Now we have passed into the realm of punitive discharges— ones that clearly label your military experience as unsatisfactory. A bad-conduct discharge is a result of a conviction in a court-martial and is roughly equivalent to a misdemeanor or minor criminal conviction in civilian life.

Again, the V.A. decides on a case-by-case basis if the holder gets any benefits, but with a bad-conduct discharge the deck is stacked against you.

Dishonorable Discharge

This is the worst discharge a military person can receive. It indicates that you have been convicted of a serious crime—one that might be considered a felony outside the armed forces.

This ultimate "bad paper" strips the holder of most of the veterans' benefits, and in some states he or she will even lose the right to vote. Getting a job with a dishonorable discharge is extremely difficult.

The five grades of discharge are clearly established but the conditions that result in each one aren't. Discharges are a tool for the military, and different branches (and different commanders) use them in varying ways.

The discharge system first of all encourages military personnel to work hard and do a good job. The promise of benefits after leaving the service is enough to motivate people, and the threat of a bad discharge and the consequences that follow help to keep most military personnel in line.

The second function of the discharge system is to make it easy to get rid of people who cannot or will not function in a military setting. Slight physical or mental disorders could prove life-threatening in a combat situation, both to the person with the disorder and those around.

As for those who will not function, the armed services tolerate a narrow range of behavior, and characteristics that might be considered acceptable or even admirable in civilian life—such as nonconformity or spontaneity—do not work in a military setting. The armed forces function best when unimpeded, and those who go against the flow may find themselves heading for a discharge.

You cannot apply for discharge under most of the conditions that lead to it. There is no form, for example, to tell your commander that you have a behavioral disorder. The military assumes that such a condition will be obvious to the authorities.

There are some situations, however, where an enlisted person can apply for special consideration by the military. They include, but are not limited to, hardship, dependency, erroneous enlistment, and conscientious objector status.

Dependency

Sue is ten years older than her brother. She joins the Air Force, and, while stationed in Greenland, learns that both her parents have been killed in an auto accident. She is the only relative her twelve-year-old brother has.

Sue can apply for a dependency discharge. An application and supporting documents must generally be submitted to the commanding officer, who forwards them to the proper authorities. Sometimes the applicant is interviewed for further information, but often the documents that accompany the application are enough.

Usually a person who applies for discharge due to dependency receives an honorable or a general discharge, depending on his or her record.

Hardship

While Roger is serving in the Navy his unemployed father falls off a ladder and breaks his back. The resulting medical bills force the family, of which Roger is the only child, into near bankruptcy. Even the money that Roger sends home is insufficient to pull the family through.

Roger can apply for a hardship discharge. As with Sue's dependency situation, an application must be filled out and accompanied by documentation that supports the claim. This sort of discharge is more difficult to achieve with the advent of social service funds such as Medicare, Medicaid, food stamps, and so on.

As with the dependency situation, the person who is approved for hardship status generally receives an honorable or general discharge.

Erroneous Enlistment

Hernando joins the Navy to be an air traffic controller. He asks his recruiter to make sure he is qualified for the training before he signs up. He is assured in writing that he is qualified for air traffic control training, and he enlists.

However, with 20/200 corrected vision, Hernando is not qualified for air traffic control school, and when it is learned that he had relatives in Cuba it becomes obvious that he probably would never get the security clearance to become a military air traffic controller.

Hernando is a good candidate for an erroneous enlistment discharge. Anyone receiving a written guarantee of training is entitled to get it or be discharged. (This is another good reason to get all of the recruiter's promises in writing. If they were only spoken, Hernando would have a very hard time making his case.)

A person in such a situation should prepare a statement requesting discharge and explaining the problem. As with any application for discharge, any and all supporting documents, such as the recruiting contract, should be included. (This is a good reason to always keep a copy of anything you sign.)

If Hernando is successful in his quest he will receive an honorable discharge. Then his recruiter will have to sweat.

Conscientious Objector

When you enlist in the armed forces, one of the questions on the form that you sign asks: "Do you now have, or have you ever had, a firm, fixed, and sincere objection to participation in war of any form or to the bearing of arms because of religious training or belief ?" If you answer yes it will not necessarily prevent you from applying for enlistment, but it is doubtful that you will be accepted into the military.

Even after you have answered the question with a no, military officials recognize that while in uniform you may develop a conscientious objection to war or the bearing of arms. They don't like it, but they recognize it.

A person may become a conscientious objector (C.O.) in several ways. Some become C.O.'s after experiencing combat or being ordered into combat. The young woman who entered the military to gain a job skill or money for college may realize with a shock that the B-52 bomber she is repairing carries nuclear weapons. Or the recruit on the Marine rifle range may realize that he is being trained to shoot at human beings.

However you become a C.O., you can get an honorable discharge from the military. To do so you must convince the authorities that you came to your C.O. beliefs after entering the military. You do not have to be a member of a church—you don't even have to believe in God—nor do you have to renounce the use of force in all situations.

All of the services have procedures for filing for a C.O. discharge. It is not complicated, but it takes time and a lot of perseverance. You must prepare to undergo isolation and perhaps some abuse from those around you. But it can be done. Since 1970, according to the Central Committee for Conscientious Objectors (CCCO), an organization that assists persons applying for C.O. status, almost ten thousand military members have applied for C.O. discharges and over six thousand have been granted.

The CCCO advises talking to a civilian counselor before initiating the procedures. He or she can help you think through your position clearly and advise you on the best way to proceed. For further information write or call the CCCO, 2016 Walnut Street, Philadelphia, Pennsylvania 19103.

14. Women in the Military

O NE OF THE BIGGEST CHANGES to hit the military has been the active recruitment of women. Females have served in uniform for a long time, but until ten years ago their activities were for the most part confined to traditional jobs such as nursing or working in an office.

Now women can be found serving as crew chiefs for F-16s and electronics specialists in the Navy, and stationed beside men in the Army in Europe. Great strides have been made since the 1973 change, but neither the service nor the women in it have entirely adjusted to the situation. Women in uniform still face special problems.

History

The role of women in combat has varied drastically over the past three hundred years. Recent wars have conditioned Americans not to associate women with combat. Females have on occasion found themselves in action—when hospitals were attacked, for example—but for the most part they have been kept away from fighting.

This was not always the case. In colonial days, when isolated settlements were attacked by Indians, anyone who could fire a rifle did so, and women as well as men took up positions in forts and stockades.

This early tradition of women fighting alongside men gradually evolved into one of women serving as camp followers. In the ragtag armies of the revolutionary war women came along to work as nurses, cooks, and laundresses. But more than a few took part in the fighting. The most famous of these is Molly Pitcher, who filled in for her wounded husband on a cannon crew and eventually was welcomed into the army by George Washington.

Several women took part in battles, some on an emergency basis like Molly Pitcher and others who volunteered for full-time duty. Some went so far as to dress like men in order to join. This pattern continued through the War of 1812 and even into the Civil War, when women took part in combat on both sides.

Although it marked the end of women's participation in combat, the Civil War also marked the beginning of efforts to organize the camp followers. Abraham Lincoln authorized Clara Barton to create a regiment of women nurses. In 1901 Congress formally established the Army Nurse Corps, and the Navy Nurse Corps followed in 1908. Despite the fact that they were part of the armed forces, these nurses could not hold rank, nor were they entitled to the same benefits as men.

In World War I women began to move out of the hospitals and into administrative posts to free men for combat. This time around they were given rank and were officially discharged when the war was over. Over one hundred thirty thousand women served in this capacity in World War I.

The role of women in World War II was considerably expanded with the creation of the Women's Army Corps (WAC), the Navy's Women Accepted for Volunteer Emergency Service (WAVES), the Women Airforce Service Pilots (WASP), and the Marine Corps and Coast Guard Women's Reserve. Two hundred sixty-five thousand women were in uniform during the war, and their duties included flying new aircraft to the front, instructing men in basic training, and the usual clerking and nursing.

Although an effort was made to keep women out of combat, many were present where fighting took place. Nurses were taken prisoner by the Japanese, and other women—like their frontier ancestors—picked up guns and fought alongside the men when things got desperate. On the home front, civilian women proved that they could handle difficult factory jobs once limited to men.

By 1948 the authorities were convinced that there was a permanent role for females in the armed forces, and women were allowed to enlist in active units and the reserves. Limits were placed on the total number of women who could join up and the rank they could attain, and they were specifically barred from flying combat aircraft or serving on naval combat vessels. Oddly enough, the law did not prevent them from fighting on the ground, although an internal Army policy accomplished that.

Women served with distinction in Korea, but it wasn't until Vietnam that their numbers in the military rose significantly. The ceiling on the number of women in uniform was lifted, and close to one hundred ninety-three thousand women were on duty during those years. Approximately seventy-five hundred actually went to Vietnam, mostly as nurses.

Then came the end of the draft in 1973. The country was disenchanted with military service, primarily because of Vietnam, and the various branches of the armed forces had to scramble to meet enlistment quotas. For the first time they began to recruit women in nontraditional fields. There were approximately fifty-five thousand females on active duty in 1973, and this number rose to 111,753 in 1976 and 184,651 in 1981. Currently there are approximately 190,230 women in uniform.

With their numbers increasing so quickly, pressure was brought to admit women into the service academies.

Traditionalists in every branch fought the move and male cadets huffed and puffed about how women would never be able to take the physical and psychological pressures that mark academy life.

Congress disagreed, however, and in 1976 women were admitted to the academies. These female cadets were subjected to intense scrutiny by the media, and whenever one would drop out the papers would carry a story. But most of them prevailed; they graduated and were commissioned as officers. Although there is still grumbling in some quarters about women in the academies, most people consider the change a success.

With women so firmly a part of the nation's armed forces, a growing number of voices inside and outside the military are arguing that women should take part in combat. An equally vociferous group insists this should never take place. If the restrictions against combat are ever dropped, the women in the American military will take their place alongside their male counterparts much as their pioneer ancestors did. They will have come full circle at last.

Things Women Should Consider

Aside from the usual questions confronting someone who is considering military service—what branch to join, whether to become an officer or enlisted person and the like—women have additional matters to consider. Society does not always prepare women for the performance expected in a military setting. Once in uniform, females may encounter problems caused by physical differences, the military institutions themselves, and the men in uniform.

Just like their male counterparts, some women go through the military with a minimum of bother, while others are miserable from day one. Before you sign the enlistment papers, here are a few things you should think about.

Reactions in the civilian world. The woman who announces to her family and friends that she is enlisting in the armed forces will get a reaction different from that a man would get.

"I didn't know you were that desperate" is a comment often heard. Some people see the military as an employer of last resort and assume that a woman is at the end of her rope when she joins.

Others imagine that the only reason a woman would join the military is to find a husband. A smaller group will accuse an enlistee—though not to her face—of being promiscuous or of having no self-esteem. And a minority may mutter comments about her being a lesbian.

Close friends or others who would snort at the above accusations will often question how a young woman could involve herself with anything involving war and destruction. They see this as an exclusively male activity and wonder why a woman, who is trained by society to be a nurturer, would want any part of it.

You can't prevent someone from making negative remarks about whatever you do, whether it is joining a religious order or flying an Army helicopter. That's part of life. You can, however, talk to people about your own feelings regarding military service. Present or former servicewomen can give you some good advice, or at least explain how they resolved the issue. If nothing else, they may supply you with a quick line to squelch those folks who inevitably sniff that "the military is no place for a girl."

Physical differences. When women first started filling nontraditional roles in the military, they found that the uniforms and boots and pieces of equipment they were supposed to use were not suited for women's bodies. These problems have largely been worked out by now, but the physical differences between men and women are still very evident in some quarters.

Women have less upper body strength than men, and this can make basic training very difficult. Despite special exercises and standards, women still find holding a rifle and performing drills with it particularly hard. Most men have had some practice at throwing and do not have the problems with grenades that many women have. And women are hard put to climb ropes and upright barriers as easily as men.

In the summer of 1982 the Army announced it was going to test women to make sure they could perform certain jobs requiring great muscular strength. This was in part a reaction to complaints from the field that women weren't always able to pull their share of the load. This physical difference may limit the number of skills you can qualify for.

Finally, men are not always understanding and sensitive regarding the problems some women suffer with menstrual periods. Trying to explain severe cramps to a male drill instructor or commanding officer may be embarrassing and frustrating.

Jobs and career. The law against flying combat aircraft and being on Navy combat ships, plus the Army's policy of keeping women out of jobs that could entail combat duty in a war, can have a tremendous impact on your military experience.

For one thing, it means you will not have as large a selection of jobs as will a man. Even if you are admitted into a certain job classification, you might not be able to perform your duties because you cannot go where the work is done.

Many women who talk to Army recruiters are surprised to learn that since 1982 females have been barred from building trades such as interior electrical work, plumbing, carpentry, and masonry. The Army justified this move by pointing out that these are "combat engineering skills." An interior electrician, for example, in addition to installing lights and switches, "lays and clears minefields, primes and emplaces explosives and demolitions, constructs and removes wires, beach and river obstacles. . . ."[1] This runs counter to promises of learning a useful career in the Army.

All of the services will guarantee your training, but none will promise you the job you train for. If your particular plans don't materialize, your commanding officer—who will probably be male—is free to put you where he needs you. And if he is one of those men who thinks that only woman can type or file or perform some other traditionally feminine job, you may find

---

1. Nora Scott Kinzer, letter to the editor, *New York Times*, August 24, 1982.

yourself doing the sort of thing you joined the service to escape.

The ban on combat can be a hindrance to the woman who is in only for a few years, but it can be a serious obstacle for those who wish to make the military a career. An officer must have had a few kinds of experience in order to compete for the top-level positions. In the Navy, for example, this means commanding a ship. Women can command a few types of vessels, but they are usually the less exciting ones—certainly not aircraft carriers or destroyers.

And if a war or skirmish breaks out, the officers in a combat area have an opportunity to demonstrate their leadership under fire. This path of advancement is closed to women, and makes their assumption of the higher ranks much less likely. The situation may change in the future, but you should make your plans assuming it won't.

Sexual harassment. According to the Department of Defense's definition, sexual harassment can range from obscene comments or gestures to sexual contact. It is perhaps the worst problem a woman will face in the armed forces.

The situation is not so much an institutional as an individual problem. From the Secretary of Defense on down, each of the armed forces deplores sexual harassment and has issued countless memorandums on the subject. If a clear-cut case comes to their attention, they usually move quickly to discipline the guilty party.

Sexual harassment can take many forms. The man who constantly uses obscene language or tells sexual jokes in your presence is guilty of sexual harassment. The person who constantly asks for a date even though you have made it clear you aren't interested is guilty of sexual harassment. And the officer who suggests that going to bed with him is the only way you will get promoted is certainly guilty of sexual harassment.

Witnessing or being a victim of sexual harassment is one thing, but getting anything done about it is something else. The problem stems mainly from the rank system—the chain of command. The person commanding you has considerable power over you. He can influence your advancement, your assignments, and even small matters such as your leaves and liberties.

Sexual harassment can easily take place given this power of one person over another. And the arrangement that makes it easy to happen makes it difficult to punish. If you want to make a complaint about sexual harassment you have to go to the person above you. And if he is the culprit, you have to go to the officer above him. Jumping the chain of command is rarely done in the military, and making this move takes a lot of courage.

Assuming you accuse the officer above you of sexual harassment, how can you prove it? Most sexual demands are not made in public, and it may simply be your word against his. If the superior officer decides to drop the matter or rules in favor of the offender, you are still under the accused's command—and may be in hot water. Women sometimes fear they are in physical danger after making an accusation of sexual harassment.

The outright sexual invitation or threat is an example of serious harassment, but sometimes the little things are the most pervasive and irritating. The *Stars and Stripes*, a newspaper for military personnel, ran an article in 1982 detailing cases of sexual harassment in American military communities in Europe. One woman stopped eating in the mess hall because of the constant leers and comments. She described it as "an unpleasant, anxiety-producing experience."[2]

What should women do? Another *Stars and Stripes* article suggests confronting the offender and asking him to stop. If this doesn't work, the victim should report the incident to the next person in the chain of command, an equal opportunity officer, or a women's advocacy officer. The story ends with a promising quote from an Army researcher: "There's a growing number of commanders out there who want to do something about the sexual harassment problem. But there's nothing they can do if women don't report it."[3]

---

2. *Stars and Stripes*, July 23, 1982.
3. *Stars and Stripes*, July 21, 1982.

Some women can shrug off sexual harassment, while others are driven to leave the military because of it. You should consider how you would react to this unfortunate aspect of military service. It shows little sign of going away soon.

Family life. Family life in the armed forces is certainly not just a woman's concern, but matters such as a two-career marriage and pregnancy are of particular concern to women considering the military.

A family begins with a marriage. There is a fair possibility you may decide to marry someone in your branch of the service—over forty-five thousand couples have done so. Just as in civilian marriages, military couples have to make decisions about which career paths to follow. Staying together can be difficult if your spouse has a combat job and gets stationed in areas where you cannot go. Making sure you stay together can limit job possibilities and affect advancement—yours and his.

Marriage to someone in another branch of the service is possible, but that really makes things complicated. And if you marry a civilian, he may not appreciate being dragged from base to base and job to job.

Children complicate matters further. The armed forces used to regard pregnancy as grounds for automatic discharge, but this is no longer the case. You can request discharge if you want, and it will be granted. If you want to stay in the military after having the child, you are usually guaranteed no special consideration in assignments or station duties based solely on the fact tht you are a parent. Unless medical conditions dictate otherwise, you are expected to be back in the saddle six weeks after delivery.

As children grow older, a military life can mean changing schools every year, constantly making and leaving friends, and perhaps showing deference to the children of those who outrank you. Thousands of children have been raised as military dependents; some of them thrived or at least didn't suffer from the experience, whereas others truly earned the title "military brat."

Outlook

The WAVES and the WACs and the WASPs of World War II days are long gone, but the attitudes that keep women on a pedestal—albeit an olive-drab one—are still very much in place in the armed forces.

As mentioned elsewhere in this book, the military is sometimes a few steps behind society as a whole, and as far as women are concerned this is clearly the case. Whether and how quickly the service will follow society is difficult to predict.

In some respects now is a good time to be a woman in uniform. As commanders strive to show that their unit is on a par with the rest of the branch, they tend to favor women with promotions, special programs, and anything that will help females achieve a highly visible role. Fair or not, it's great to be on the receiving end of this treatment.

The ban on combat jobs still frustrates the short-termer as well as the career woman in the armed forces. The failure of the Equal Rights Amendment insured that the ban can stay in place until Congress decides to lift it. Given the effectiveness of right-wing interest groups, it is unlikely that this ban will be lifted anytime soon.

In the ten years that women have been in the nontraditional parts of the armed forces, tremendous progress has been made. The next ten years may see a similar move toward reducing sexual harassment, eliminating the ban on combat, and moving closer in every way to a fighting force that uses the full abilities of its members, whether male or female.

In the meantime you should keep in mind that the benefits of military service come with some not-so-small problems. Since the situation varies from branch to branch, the best way to find out which branch is best for you is to sit down and talk with a woman who has been in uniform—not a recruiter—and who can tell you the straight story.

15. Blacks in the Military

MINORITIES AND THE MILITARY constitute a study in contrasts. On one hand the armed forces, through their training and benefits, offer some of the best ways to rise out of a life of poverty and discrimination. On the other hand they can subject a young person to some of the most hateful racism he or she will ever encounter.

Even the history of minorities—particularly blacks—in the armed forces has shown vast swings. For decades the numbers of blacks were purposely kept low, and they were confined to the most menial tasks. Then, in a complete turnaround, the Department of Defense became the first major American institution to be integrated. Now some observers feel there are too many minority members in some of the services.

A prominent sociologist who has studied the military once stated, "I'd say that racism—the American dilemma—is *the* problem of all the armed services, wherever the troops are." Yet he added, "I believe the military has gone further in attacking racism than any other institution our society has."[1]

History

The role of blacks in American military history roughly parallels that of women. Blacks went from fighting alongside whites to serving as camp followers, then working in support positions before finally taking their place again in all aspects of combat.

Most histories of blacks in combat begin with Crispus Attucks, the first American to die in the infamous Boston Massacre of 1770. Black citizen-soldiers fought beside their white counterparts at Lexington and Concord. They took part in nearly every engagement of war, sometimes on both sides. Not surprisingly, considering the slaveholding policies of the colonials, more blacks fought for the British than for the revolutionaries.

After the Revolution the young United States took steps to relegate blacks—like women—to the status of camp followers. Despite this, close to a thousand blacks saw action in the War of 1812. Most were excluded from the armed service, however, and those permitted to join served officially as cooks or servants.

This state of affairs remained until the middle of the Civil War, when the North realized it had a valuable untapped resource. Several all-black companies were established, and after the Emancipation Proclamation of 1863 volunteers readily filled the special regiments. Over seven thousand blacks were commissioned as officers, although most of these were doctors or chaplains. When the war was almost over even the South saw fit to allow blacks to join up and fight. (There is

---

1. Bruce Bliven, Jr., *Volunteers, One and All* (New York: Reader's Digest Press, 1976), pp. 120-21.

no record, however, of many availing themselves of this privilege).

Having proven themselves in action, black units were maintained and sent to the West where they fought with the Indians. They became so proficient at cavalry tactics that two black units accompanied Teddy Roosevelt in the famous attack on San Juan Hill in Cuba during the Spanish-American War.

Despite their demonstrated willingness and readiness to fight for their country, "World War I saw official armed forces policy toward blacks at its worst—rigid segregation, partial exclusion, and open and virulent racism on the part of numerous white commanders of black units."[2] So writes one historian. Combat-trained black troops were put to work as laborers or cooks. Even during this low in minority-military relations, however, one black unit—the 370th Regiment, one of the few with black commanders—performed superbly and was highly decorated.

But after the war it was back to segregation as usual. Black soldiers in the Army could not serve in the Air Corps or the artillery, engineers, signal, or tank corps; and the Navy and Marines kept their blacks safely in the kitchen.

World War II marked the beginning of the change. Much as in the Civil War, blacks were not utilized at first. Like the women in uniform, blacks found themselves in support positions instead of combat. They unloaded ships, drove trucks, and took their usual positions in kitchens and servant quarters.

When manpower shortages occurred late in the war, blacks were taken out of the support positions and sent to the front. A new Naval Secretary, James Forrestal, integrated basic and advanced training, put ten-percent-black crews on certain ships, and commissioned the first black naval officers.

Many blacks who participated in the fighting distinguished themselves; several units were highly decorated, and

---

2. Richard J. Stillman II, "Black Participation in the Armed Forces," in *Black American Reference Book*, Mabel Smythe, ed. (Englewood Cliffs, N. J.: Prentice Hall, 1976), p. 894. Much of the material in this chapter comes from Stillman's excellent work.

generals such as George Patton spoke highly of the black troops under his command.

But there were still segregated units, and their members were forced to endure separate officer clubs, noncommissioned officers' clubs, and recreation facilities. The Red Cross even established a separate blood bank for blacks. Only this time the blacks didn't take it sitting down. When they were treated unfairly by white officers they complained, and sometimes they went further. Riots broke out at Army bases in Hawaii, Georgia, and Louisiana, and the Navy experienced serious racial clashes at ports in San Francisco and Guam.

The change was long overdue, and in the late forties the segregational barriers began to crumble. President Harry Truman signed an executive order that established equal treatment and opportunity for all persons in the armed services. The newly created Air Force set the pace by complying with the order first; the Navy made impressive gains, while the Army held onto its segregated units.

It took the war in Korea to bring the Army into line. Blacks enlisted in large numbers, and it was impossible to put all of them into the special units. By the end of the war the armed forces were entirely integrated—the first major institution in the country to become so.

Despite the advances made on an institutional level, blacks in the armed forces still faced problems during the Vietnam years. Unlike in earlier wars in which they had initially been kept away from combat, blacks, many of whom had been drafted against their will, fought in disproportionately large numbers in Vietnam. This was a matter of contention nationwide; many people felt black troops were bearing the brunt of the fighting while whites were sitting at home with student deferments.

Other issues surfaced during and immediately after the Vietnam period. The rise of black militancy and a corresponding unwillingness to tolerate racism led to barracks battles at military installations and on ships. A few white troops organized Ku Klux Klan chapters, and tensions ran high. One German employee of the Army in Europe offered this analysis:

"In the Volunteer Army you are recruiting the best of the blacks and the worst of the whites."[3] This was clearly an exaggeration, but it contained a kernel of truth.

Whatever the problems, military service continues to hold great appeal for minority men and women. The racism in the armed forces is now more on an individual level than an institutional one, and efforts are being made to weed it out. Courses on "human relations" are taught to every officer and enlistee—an educational task unparalleled in the United States. The situation is vastly better than it was twenty years ago, yet there are still some things blacks should consider before deciding to join the armed forces.

Things Blacks Should Consider

Military service makes unique demands on a person. You are expected to obey orders without question, to take abuse and not reply, and to show respect and follow the commands of any person who outranks you. And you can't quit.

Furthermore, in a military setting you may be thrown into close contact with people you would normally not associate with. You may have to work or even live with a person who does not share your viewpoint. Despite the human relations courses, despite the attention paid to racial matters, and despite the countless letters and memorandums circulated on the subject, there are still out-and-out racists in uniform. They may be in your company. Worse yet, they may be in charge of your company. You have to learn to deal with these people without detracting from your goals in the military. It isn't always easy. Here are some questions you should ask yourself.

Racism: can I handle it? If you grew up in an all-black neighborhood and attended high school with lots of your friends, you may never have encountered some of the more ugly forms of racism. You may never have had a white person call you "nigger" to your face. How will you react if this

---

3. Brent Scowcroft, ed. *Military Service in the United States* (Englewood Cliffs, N. J.: Prentice Hall, 1982), p. 133.

happens? Will you get into a fight? Report the incident? Or try to get back at the person?

If a white person gets a job you were qualified for or a promotion you should have had, what will you do? Will you let it eat away at your insides, gradually filling you with hate? Will you throw up your hands and give up, sullenly marking time until you are discharged? Or will you work harder so you will get the job or the promotion next time?

In thinking about joining the armed forces, you have to look at yourself as well as the enlistment options. You may come to the conclusion that you would not operate well in a military setting; it's a lot better to recognize this *before* you get in.

What if I am assigned to a tough duty station? Most people assume that when they join the service there will always be some place to go on the weekends, people to meet—particularly of the opposite sex—and opportunities for good times. The brochures in recruiting offices often picture racially mixed groups having a party on a beach, sitting in a nice restaurant, or skiing down a mountainside. This isn't always the way it is. You may be assigned to a base near a town in the boondocks where there are no minorities. The only place to go on Saturday night may be the Redneck Dew Drop Inn. Or you may be overseas where no one off the base speaks English and those on base want nothing to do with you.

Many men and women on duty in places like Korea or Germany find themselves hanging around the base during their leave time. Cheap drinks in the club or readily available drugs can lead to trouble. Tensions sometimes run high in situations like this, and often minority groups and whites find themselves at odds. Off-base housing may be an answer, but it may not be available for minorities or may be so expensive that it might as well not be there at all. And you could be stationed in such a place for more than a year.

In considering this possibility, you should examine the various branches of the service and find out where you might be stationed. In selecting your job training, inquire of the recruiter where such jobs are most often done. Ask if there is a base-of-choice or country-of-choice option.

Can I get a better deal in the military than as a civilian ? This question is the bottom line, and there's no way of definitely answering it until you're in. And by then it's too late to back out.

The military still poses a lot of problems for minorities. Racism still exists. Blacks are imprisoned in military stockades at a higher rate than whites. There is a greater proportion of white officers, and blacks are more often found shouldering a rifle than learning a technical skill. Minorities are more likely than whites to receive a dishonorable discharge. Some black veterans are extremely bitter about their treatment in the armed forces, and quite a few feel they are worse off for the experience.

Yet the potential for bettering yourself is there. Despite the racism and raw deals—which aren't unheard of in civilian life—you can go into the armed forces with nothing and come out with a useful skill or money that will help you go to school and make something of yourself. For many people the military was the first break on the way to success. If you can put up with the hassles and the unpleasant people, if you can work in spite of the adversity, the service can be the best thing that can happen to you.

The smartest thing to do before signing the enlistment papers is to talk to a minority veteran or someone who is still in uniform. Ask them the hard questions; get them to tell you about their good and bad experiences. Don't talk only to recruiters—even black ones. Things must have gone well for them, or they wouldn't be behind that desk.

If you decide to go into the service, at least you'll enlist with a clear idea of what to expect—good things and bad.

16. Educational and Post-Service Benefits

PERHAPS THE MOST SOUGHT-AFTER benefits of military service are educational. Money for education is available before, during, and after active duty. Once you are back in civilian clothes you are eligible for other benefits as well: veterans are sometimes favored in hiring decisions, and you may be entitled to a pension, a loan guarantee, and free medical care.

EDUCATION IN THE ARMED FORCES

By and large the military authorities have always felt that educated military personnel make up a superior force. Such people can be trained more quickly, can operate complicated weapons more effectively, and, when properly motivated, can fight better.

For these reasons the armed forces have long encouraged their troops to obtain knowledge. The General Education Development Test (GED)—the high school equivalency test—originated in the military, and millions of classroom hours have been logged under military supervision.

Since the end of the draft, however, education has reached an even higher priority. You can still complete your high school work in the military, but now opportunities exist for taking college courses, obtaining a master's degree, and even going to medical school.

All this emphasis on education serves three important functions for the armed service. First, it brings in good people. Those with little schooling and few skills have always gravitated to the military, but increased money for education brings in the best recruits—men and women who are top-flight. With tuition costs rising and opportunities for getting loans declining, the educational benefits appeal to just the kind of people the armed forces want.

Second, money for education helps keep good people in the armed forces. Officers who are sent to graduate or professional schools incur a longer obligation to serve and stand a better chance of being promoted. The longer a person stays in, the more likely he or she will remain until retirement—an outcome the military finds desirable.

Finally, the leaders in the armed forces feel that money spent for education will benefit the services as a whole. Sending men and women into the civilian world to learn the latest in technological and managerial techniques can help the armed forces to perform more efficiently and effectively.

What's in It for Me?

From an individual's point of view, there are distinct advantages in taking up the military's offer of education in exchange for service. Unlike civilian scholarships, which usually demand applicants with the highest grades, the military has money for students at varying levels of ability. And there are several ways of getting that money.

Some people, such as academy cadets or ROTC scholar-ship recipients, go for the education before they enter active duty. This "go to school now, pay later" plan allows you to go to college right after high school and thus avoid interrupting your schooling. You spend the years in uniform later.

Others opt for a "pay now, go to school later" plan whereby they join up, complete their hitch, and then go to school. In this manner they can go straight from college into the job market without having to spend several years in the service. Unlike academy or ROTC members, veterans can choose any course of study whatsoever as long as it is offered in an approved institution. What was once known as the G.I. Bill, now called the Veteran's Education Assistance Program (VEAP), will be discussed more thoroughly later in this chapter, under Post-Service Benefits.

A third group decides to "go to school now and pay now." They enlist or join the officer corps and work at getting an education while in uniform. This plan has several benefits, the biggest of which is the money you save. If you are working towards a college degree, the military will pay up to 90 percent of the tuition for courses taken during off-duty hours. Officers can attend graduate or even medical school for free; this is worth thousands of dollars in tuition and other costs.

The more education you receive the more likely you are to be promoted. Often schooling qualifies you for advanced duties, and it may be a means for enlisted personnel to make the jump to the officer corps. And if you plan to finish college after being discharged, any courses you complete while in uniform will be ones you won't have to take when you get out.

Going to school in the military has its problems as well as its promises. Courses are usually taken on your own time; this isn't always easy in the service, where people often work longer than forty hours per week. Furthermore, your courses have to be approved by your commanding officer and must be useful in some way to the military.

People in the armed forces tend to move around a lot, and this can be frustrating for someone who is trying to graduate from a particular college. Every branch has ways of transferring credits to a central institution, whether a military or a civilian one, but most of these places are junior colleges or community colleges; there are no "name" schools on the list.

If the service sends you to graduate school or medical school you incur a long obligation, as much as three years in uniform for every one year in school. Like so many other things in the armed forces, the educational benefits are part of a trade-off. You should look at your own situation, consider the possibilities carefully, and see if the advantages outweigh the disadvantages.

Education Before Active Duty

Service academies and ROTC scholarships are covered in Chapter 11.

Education During Active Duty

The widest range of educational possibilities is offered while you are in uniform. Some programs are common to all the branches, and others are unique to one branch or another. Keep in mind that educational benefits change from time to time; check with your local recruiter if you have any questions about a particular one.

The programs described below are offered to enlistees or officers who have been in uniform for less than four years. Each branch of the service has options for personnel who are further along their career path, but these will not be covered here.

Across-the-Board Benefits

☐ *DANTES.* This stands for Defense Activity for Non-traditional Education Support, an agency that provides opportunities to take tests and transfer experience into credits that are recognized by civilian colleges. Among other things, DANTES offers the GED test, the ACT and SAT exams needed to apply for college, and the Graduate Record Exam (GRE) required for graduate school.

☐ *Tuition Assistance Program.* If you are on active duty the military will pay up to 90 percent of tuition fees for off-duty courses on the college level. (The Coast Guard pays $200 per semester.) There is no obligation for enlisted personnel, but officers incur a two-year obligation (one year in the Coast Guard).

☐ *Serviceman's Opportunity College.* This is designed to help active-duty personnel earn a college degree or certificate while they are being transferred from place to place. Several hundred four-year and two-year colleges enroll military personnel and record their credits as they take courses in various places.

☐ Any *Scholarships, Fellowships, and Grants* that you might win in your academic career are almost always honored by the armed forces. This could mean that you could spend a year in this country or abroad furthering your studies while in the service.

☐ *Uniformed Services University: The School of Medicine.* is the armed forces' place to become a doctor. It costs you nothing, but you incur a seven-year obligation when you finish.

Army Benefits

☐ *The Army Continuing Education System* is available to all active-duty personnel. It provides academic, vocational, and technical services at little or no cost. These services may include help in getting your high school diploma and college preparatory classes as well as job-oriented courses.

☐ *The Army College Fund* is one of the best educational deals in the armed forces. It works like this: you choose from a special list of jobs—many of which are combat specialties—and the Army gives you a bonus. You then contribute a portion of your salary into a fund, and the government contributes twice that amount. The total amount is available for your education.

If you sign up for two years you receive an $8,000 bonus. If you have the allowable maximum of $100 (approximately one-sixth of a private's wages) deducted from your paycheck, by the time you get out you will have saved $2,400. The government will add twice that, or $4,800, for a total of $7,200. Add in the $8,000 bonus and you have $15,200 for college, and you've only served two years' active duty.

If you decide you want more, you can enlist for three years' active duty and come out with $20,100. If you stay in for four years, you wind up with $25,100.

□ *The Health Profession Scholarship Program* will pay your way through civilian medical school and give you money to live on while you become a doctor. Once you're out you owe the Army one year for every year you were in this program.

□ *The Fully Funded Legal Education Program* is just what the name says; they will pay your way through law school. You have to be an officer with at least two but no more than six years of active duty at the time the schooling begins.

Navy Benefits

□ *The Campus High School Studies Program* is available to enlisted personnel who want to get their high school diplomas. Classes are offered during working hours in English, math, reading, and other subjects and can lead to a diploma or successful completion of the GED.

□ In the *Navy College Degree Program* an active-duty officer can finish a bachelor of science degree in eighteen months or less of full-time attendance at a civilian school. You get paid your regular wages by the Navy, but you have to pay for the schooling. You incur an obligation of one year for every six months of study.

□ *The Program for Afloat College Education* enables you to take tuition-free college courses while on ships at sea. Most of the courses are at the freshman or sophomore level, and all are offered by accredited colleges, whose professors ship out with you.

☐ *The Secretary of the Navy Scholarship* allows officers to go to civilian colleges to take courses that are useful to the Navy. The obligation is three times the length of the educational program.

Air Force Benefits

☐ *The Airman Education and Commissioning Program* enables enlisted personnel to join the officer corps. You have to have earned forty-five semester hours in college with a 2.0 (C) average, and you must be less than thirty-five years old when commissioned. You are sent to college to get a bachelor of science degree in a scientific or technical discipline, and then you go to OTS. You must commit yourself to six years in the Air Force when you enter the program and four years upon commissioning as an officer.

☐ *Bootstrap Temporary Duty* assigns you to full-time study at a civilian college for up to one year while you complete a bachelor of science degree. They pay your regular wages but you pay for the schooling, and once you finish you owe the Air Force three months for every one month you were in school. Following this you may apply for OTS.

☐ *The Community College of the Air Force* is the only federal agency that has the power to grant degrees. You receive academic credit for basic training and job training and then add courses taken off-duty at civilian colleges, for which the Air Force pays 90 percent of the tuition. You eventually receive an associate's degree, and no obligation is incurred.

☐ *The Extension Course Institute* is the Air Force's correspondence school. While stationed anywhere, you can choose from over four hundred courses. The school is free and open to officers and enlisted personnel.

☐ *The Engineering Conversion Program* sends college-educated officers back to college to get a second degree in engineering. All fees are paid, and you are obligated to stay in the Air Force for three times the length of your training period.

☐ *The Air Force Institute of Technology* is a graduate school situated near Dayton, Ohio, that offers programs in engineering, logistics, and subjects pertaining directly to the Air Force.

☐ *The Air Force Graduate Education Program* sends qualified officers to civilian graduate schools to receive a master's or doctoral degree. They pay your wages and all fees, and you are obligated to serve three times the length of the schooling to a maximum of four years for a master's and five years for a doctorate.

☐ *Legal Education* enables officers to go to law school at Air Force expense. The obligation is two years of service for each year of schooling to a maximum of five years.

☐ *Medical Education* enables officers to go to medical school at Air Force expense. The obligation is four years of service after internship and residency.

Marine Corps Benefits

☐ *Advanced Degree Program.* This leads to a master's degree for officers. You go to school full time for a period not to exceed eighteen months. The Marines pay you; you pay for the schooling. Your obligation is three years for one year of graduate school or four years for any portion of a second year of school.

Coast Guard

☐ *Correspondence Courses.* The Coast Guard offers courses by mail in a variety of subjects.

☐ *Advanced Electronics Associate Degree Program.* Enlisted people of E-6 rank or above are paid to go to community college for two years to receive an associate's degree in electronics. The obligation is two years of service for every year in school.

☐ *Officer Post Graduate Program.* The Coast Guard gives officers the opportunity to go to graduate school in fields that include civil engineering, physics, and law. The obligation incurred is two years for every year spent in school.

POST-SERVICE BENEFITS

The American public and Congress have traditionally felt that military personnel deserve more than just a discharge when their active duty is finished. This gratitude takes the form of veterans' benefits, which are administered by the V.A.

Not surprisingly, those who have made the military their career get the best deal. If you serve in the armed forces for twenty years, you can retire and receive a pension that equals half of your final salary. This means that some people can retire at age thirty-eight or thirty-nine, with plenty of time to move into another career, and live the rest of their working lives on a paycheck and a half. Those who stay in for thirty years can retire on 75 percent of their salary.

Veterans who have been wounded or injured while on active duty also receive favorable treatment. Besides free medical coverage, they are eligible for pensions covering various degrees of disability. If they were killed in action or while on active duty, their spouses and children receive benefits.

But you don't have to be a twenty-year member or a war hero to reap veterans' benefits. Many advantages are yours even if the only shots you ever fired were on the rifle range. Chief among these are educational and employment benefits.

Veterans' Educational Benefits

After World War II the Serviceman's Adjustment Act, commonly known as the G.I. Bill, enabled thousands of veterans to go to college.

VEAP is the current version of the G.I. Bill. Basically it works like this: you contribute up to $2,700 while in uniform, the government doubles your contribution, and you can wind up with a maximum of $8,100.

This money can be used for educational purposes for up to ten years after discharge. The V.A. will pay benefits for a maximum of thirty-six months. If you go to college full time, for example, the V.A. will divide your $8,100 by thirty-six and pay $225 a month to help with your tuition bills. This money can be used for any approved four-year or two-year college and any approved trade or technical school. If you have not used all the money at the end of the ten years, your contributions will be returned to you.

Veterans' Employment Benefits

Whether you go to college or not you can take advantage of veteran's preference, a practice whereby former service people are given special help in securing governmental jobs.

This can work a couple of ways. Applicants for many governmental jobs are required to take a civil service exam, the results of which are used to rank the people who want the position. Veterans are often given a number of points to add to their score on the test; this puts them higher on the list and makes it more likely that they will get the job. In other places simply being a veteran and qualified for the job is enough to land it.

Some employers in the private sector, particularly former servicemen, have their own versions of veteran's preference. If two job applicants are equal in every way and one of them is a veteran, he or she will get the post.

Other Benefits

The V.A. can help you obtain housing. Provided you and the house or mobile home you wish to purchase meet certain standards, the V.A. will guarantee up to 60 percent of a loan to a maximum of $27,500. This loan guarantee can sometimes be just the help needed to buy a home.

Under certain circumstances veterans are eligible for free medical care. The V.A. operates hospitals in most parts of the country. You will be admitted if space is available and you cannot pay for treatment elsewhere.

Finally, veterans can be buried in national cemeteries or receive an allowance for burial expenses elsewhere. The V.A. will also provide an American flag for the funeral and a headstone or grave marker.

VAN DUSEN

17. A Final Choice

The Draft

IN TALKING ABOUT ENLISTMENTS, officer training and everything else, this book has so far limited its concern to people who *want* to enter the armed forces. All young men who reach the age of eighteen, however, must consider the military for one reason—the draft.

A revival of the draft is a hot topic among military leaders, governmental figures, and the general public. Some people see registration as the first step toward an inevitable revival of the draft. Whether this is the case remains to be seen. Enlistments have generally been running high in all of the services, and there seem to be no shortages of men and women who are willing to serve. And the country is at peace.

Some doubt that there will ever be a need for as many people as were called up in World Wars I and II. The reason is simple: if the superpowers ever decide to go to war it will all be over in a few hours with an exchange of nuclear weapons.

But that's not to say that a draft will never take place. If economic conditions and employment prospects improve, people may find military service less appealing, whatever the bonuses and benefits. Then, too, those benefits cost money, and military spending could be reduced if young people were compelled to serve instead of being lured into uniform.

Finally, there is an egalitarian argument for a revival of the draft. The all-volunteer military has drawn people primarily from the lower economic classes; privileged people have seldom joined. Some argue that military protection is the responsibility of everyone—no matter what one's social or economic standing—and that the military would be better off with people of all classes present.

In all this discussion and uncertainty one thing is sure: the government expects young men to register for the draft at their local post offices. Once you fill out the form it is sent to the headquarters of the Selective Service. There are no deferments at this stage of the game; whether you are a pacifist or totally gung-ho, you are required to register.

Unless you are female. While feminists declare that a male-only draft is unfair, the Supreme Court ruled that it is at least constitutional. There seems to be no groundswell of opinion in favor of drafting females; those women who are interested in a military career are more concerned with seeing the ban on combat lifted.

Some people oppose registration and advise young men not to participate. These individuals and organizations reason that if enough males do not register it will be impossible for the government to prosecute them all. Whether this will happen or not is hard to say. The Selective Service System says that a compliance rate of 98 percent must be reached for the system to be considered fair and effective. The General Accounting Office of the federal government has acknowledged that over 20 percent of the eligible young men have not registered for the draft, despite governmental prosecution of some resisters.[1]

1. *New York Times*, July 28, 1982.

It remains to be seen, however, what will happen if resisters are convicted and subjected to the maximum penalties—five years in prison and a $10,000 fine.

If you decide to resist the draft or make plans to apply for conscientious objector status, peace groups advise that you do the following:

□ *Sort out your beliefs* concerning war and military service. If you are called in to explain why you are seeking conscientious objector status, you will be closely questioned about what you believe and why.

□ *Talk to a draft counselor*, who can help you arrive at a decision. He or she will be familiar with military procedures and regulations and may be a veteran or a political activist. You can locate a draft counselor by looking in the phone book, asking a minister, or contacting one of these two groups:

CCCO
An Agency for Military and Draft Counseling
2208 South Street
Philadelphia, Pennsylvania 19146
(215) 545-4626
1251 Second Avenue
San Francisco, California 94122
(415) 566-0500

American Friends Service Committee
1515 Cherry Street
Philadelphia, Pennsylvania 19102
(215) 241-7230

A draft counselor can give you the pros and cons of various plans of action. But one word of caution: much like an overzealous recruiter, who stretches the truth to sign you up, some draft counselors may push you to take a more radical stance than you might otherwise.

□ *Register with a church or political group* as a conscientious objector. This puts you on record as having these beliefs and may help you prove your case later on.

A Final Word

Military service offers a wide range of opportunities for young people. Some of the benefits are widely advertised, such as the attainment of job skills and money for education. Others aren't talked about so much, such as the chance to make fundamental changes in your life.

In considering whether or not to join, you need to examine the opportunities and yourself and find out just what you want from the military. Is it a chance to get away from home? Is it an education? Or is it a change from a boring life? Whatever your reasons, you need to look around and see if there is any other place you can satisfy your needs.

If you want to get away from home, there are jobs that involve lots of travel. If you want a good education, there are plenty of scholarships and schools where you can work your way through. These places don't have $120 million to advertise themselves every day, but you can find them.

Talk to people. Many young people never seek advice from anyone besides their contemporaries—those who have had no more experience than themselves. If you want to go to college, spend some time talking with your high school counselor. If he or she cannot help, go to the financial aid office of a local college. Or do some reading on the matter.

If you are looking for job skills, talk to people who are doing the work you want to do; find out how they got their jobs. Talk to representatives of labor unions in your area and people in unemployment offices. You might locate an apprenticeship program that does not ask you to go to boot camp and to sign up for six years.

All of this takes time and effort, and it's never easy. Some people won't take time to talk with you; others may be friendly but of little help. You may live in an area of few resources. Just the same, it's a good idea to explore all the options before talking to a recruiter. You may wind up in uniform anyway, but at least you will know you made the best choice.

When you do at last go to a recruiter, don't be in any rush to sign up. Joining the military will profoundly affect your life for the next six years. This is something you shouldn't do on the spur of the moment.

As you compare the various branches of the service and the programs they offer, seek out veterans of each and see what they have to say. Veterans will usually be more frank with you than any recruiter. Ask them what the advantages and disadvantages were for them, and get them to tell you what they would do if they were to enlist again.

Once you narrow your list down to one or two branches and begin talking about jobs, press the recruiter for more information. Don't just accept the job title and a vague description. In the Army, for example, one title among the building trades is interior electrician—something that sounds very useful in civilian life. You do inside wiring in this job, but you may also be asked to lay and clear mine fields, prime and place explosives, and perform other combat-related tasks. This is not apparent from the name of the job or the description.

Find out what it takes to get the job you are interested in. Ask about the requirements and the tests. You may find that learning the skill you want requires qualifications that you don't have. If you get this information before you go in, *you* can decide what else to try. If you are already in uniform when this is discovered, *they* decide what you will do.

In short, before you sign any papers you should have all the information you can get about where you are going, what you are going to do, and how you will do it. Try to minimize the surprises.

This book has pointed out the negative aspects of a military commitment as well as the positive ones, but you should keep in mind that the civilian world isn't perfect either. Racism and sexism exist in industry as surely as they do in boot camp, and all too often people who aren't in uniform are promised one thing and delivered another. The big difference is that with almost any civilian situation if things don't go your way you can quit. It is possible to get out of the military before your hitch is over, but it is extremely difficult to do so.

Finally, military service is just that—service to the

country. It cannot be compared to a civilian job. There are benefits and job descriptions and other similar features, but few civilian employers will ask you to do the things that the military will.

If you join the armed forces it is possible that you will be sent into combat and get seriously hurt or even killed. One only has to stand in a national cemetery and look at the rows and rows of markers to see evidence of this. Many professional military people refer to their mission as a calling. It can certainly be that—but it's not for everyone.

If you want to go into the armed forces, you owe it to yourself to make sure it's the best thing for you.

Bibliography

The descriptions of the enlistment options and officers' programs for the various branches of the service came from publications issued by the Department of Defense and, in the case of the Coast Guard, the Department of Transportation. Over a hundred brochures and pamphlets were examined, and these were supplemented by telephone conversations and written correspondence with officials at service academies and recruiting commands, and with military information officers. The descriptions of basic training came from those who conduct such exercises. Each section on a particular branch was checked for accuracy by one or more Pentagon or public information officers in that branch.

GENERAL

"Army Halting Joint Training of Male and Female Recruits." *New York Times*, October 20, 1982.
Bliven, Bruce, Jr. *Volunteers, One and All*. New York: Reader's Digest Press, 1976.

Halloran, Richard. "Lag in Draft Registration Raises Doubts that Law Can Be Enforced." *New York Times,* July 28, 1982.

Kinzer, Nora Scott. Letter to *New York Times*, August 24, 1982.

LaBrie, Richard, and McGovern, James. "Intrinsic and Extrinsic Causes of Attrition in the Selected Reserve." *Defense Management Journal,* Third Quarter, 1981.

Longcope, Kay. "R.O.T.C.'s March Back to College." *Boston Globe,* October 31, 1982.

"Military Realities and Guidance Responsibilities." Pamphlet by the Fellowship of Reconciliation. Reprinted from *Militarism Memo,* Fall 1978.

"Military Study Group Sees No Need for Draft." *New York Times,* October 19, 1982.

Molotsky, Irvin. "Tests Indicate a Decline in Navy Drug Use." *New York Times,* September 19, 1982.

"Results of Military Bonus System Questioned." *New York Times,* September 12, 1982.

Robinson, Ruth. "Prep Schools for the Military Are Flourishing." *New York Times,* November 2, 1982.

Scowcroft, Brent, ed. *Military Service in the United States.* Englewood Cliffs, New Jersey: Prentice Hall, 1982.

Serrin, William. "Army Recruiting Thrives as Economy Falters." *New York Times,* October 13, 1982.

Taylor, Stuart, Jr. "Draft Registry Case Enmeshes U.S." *New York Times,* October 25, 1982.

Wood, David, and Citron, Alan. "With Enlistments Up, Military Faces Bigger Problems." *Boston Globe,* November 4, 1982.

BARGAINING WITH A RECRUITER

"Considering Military Enlistment? Be a Good Consumer." Philadelphia: Central Committee for Conscientious Objectors, n.d.

"Military Ads Found to Be Misleading." Philadelphia: Central Committee for Conscientious Objectors, n.d.

"Nine Things to Remember." Cambridge, Mass.: American Friends Service Committee, n.d.

"Recruiter's Promises—How Good Are They?" Philadelphia: Central Committee for Conscientious Objectors, n.d.

Schipper, Henry. "Recruitment Fraud." Philadelphia: Central Committee for Conscientious Objectors, n.d. Reprinted from the *Real Paper* (Boston).

HOW TO GET OUT

U.S., Department of Defense. "Conscientious Objectors." Directive 1300.6. August 20, 1971.

Kinchy, Jerry. *Advice for Conscientious Objectors in the Armed Forces*. 4th ed. Philadelphia: Central Committee for Conscientious Objectors, 1979.

Military Counselor's Manual. Philadelphia: Central Committee for Conscientious Objectors, n.d.

WOMEN IN THE MILITARY

"Army Halting Joint Training of Male and Female Recruits." *New York Times*, October 20, 1982.

"Army to Limit Range of Women's Duties." *Boston Globe*, August 27, 1982.

Braycich, Martha Jo. "Pregnancy: It's a Military Matter." *Stars and Stripes*, July 24, 1982.

Fleming, Eddie. "Sexual Extortion Victims 'Scared.' " *Stars and Stripes*, July 21, 1982.

Fleming, Eddie. "Verbal Abuse 'Offends Human Dignity.' " *Stars and Stripes*, July 23, 1982.

Hoyer, Bob. "If I Do the Job, Promotions Will Come." *Stars and Stripes*, July 30, 1982.

Hoyer, Bob. "They're Ready to Fight for Their Country." *Stars and Stripes*, July 22, 1982.

Hoyer, Bob. "Women 'Bust a Gut' on the Job." *Stars and Stripes*, July 20, 1982.

Leepson, Marc. "Women in the Military." *Editorial Research Reports*, July 10, 1981.

"Sex Bias Is Found at V.A. Hospitals." *New York Times*, September 30, 1982.

"This Man's Army." *New York Times*, September 13, 1982.

U.S., Congress, House, Committee on Armed Services, Military Personnel Subcommittee. *Women in the Military*. 96th Con., 1st and 2nd sess. November 13, 14, 15, 16, 1979; and February 11, 1980.

BLACKS IN THE MILITARY

"Blacks in the Military: The Myth of Equal Opportunity." Phila-
   delphia: Central Committee for Conscientious Objectors, n.d.
Gottlieb, David. *Babes in Arms.* Beverly Hills: Sage Publications,
   1980.
Smythe, Mabel, ed. *The Black American Reference Book.*
   Englewood Cliffs, New Jersey: Prentice Hall, 1976.

Index